ARK Angel Manifesto

Becoming a Messenger of Hope, Peace & Deliverance in a Turbulent World

Robert W. Klassen, MA

REFRESH Your LIFE Publishing

ARK Angel Manifesto

Becoming a Messenger of Hope, Peace & Deliverance in a Turbulent World

Refresh Your LIFE Publishing
A Division of Refresh Your LIFE International

Printed in the U.S.A.
"ISBN:978-1-54393-318-5"

Cover Design
Patrick Mugosa

Acknowledgments

To my wife Rachel for being a rock of support through encouragement, prayer and a priceless sounding board.

To Warren, Kim, Patrick, Aaron, Jade, and Alyn for being an integral part of bringing this book to completion.

Most of all, to my Savior and Lord Jesus Christ for being a dispenser of LOVE, GRACE, FAVOR, DELIVERANCE and EVERY spiritual Blessing in the Heavenly realms.

Thank You for giving me YOUR righteousness so I could be free, and thank You for the Gift of Holy Spirit who empowers me on this journey called FAITH!

Thank you, Jesus for being the ARK of safety in my Turbulent Times!

CONTENTS

Forward
Introduction

Part One
Noah - The Original ARK Angel

Chapter 1	The Name	1
Chapter 2	The Culture	9
Chapter 3	The Crisis	17
Chapter 4	The Action Plan	19
Chapter 5	The Resilience	23
Chapter 6	The Results	33
Chapter 7	The New Residence	39
Chapter 8	Reflections on Spiritual Decisions	47
Chapter 9	The Rainbow	51

Part Two
The NEED for ARK Angels Today

Chapter 10	Just for Comparison Sake	67
Chapter 11	Democracy of Righteousness	87
Chapter 12	Moral Mayhem	105
Chapter 13	Political Pathology & Educational Entropy	119

Part Three
ARK Angel Manifesto

Chapter 14	Kingdom of God - ARK Construction Project	125
Chapter 15	Patience of an ARK Angel	135
Chapter 16	Commitment of an ARK Angel	137
Chapter 17	Faithfulness of an ARK Angel	157
Chapter 18	FAITH – The Heartbeat of an ARK Angel	169
Chapter 19	ARK Angels populate the Ark	179
Chapter 20	ARK Angels are Standard Bearers	193
Chapter 21	ARK Angels are Next Gen Motivated	203
Chapter 22	NOW Recruiting ARK Angels	213
	Manifesto, Confession and Blessing	217

FORWARD

Congratulation! You have taken the first step to becoming an Ark Angel. *Ark Angel Manifesto* will change your life! By picking up this book, you have taken the first step to becoming a survivor in our turbulent world. The wisdom of the ages has said, "a picture is worth a thousand words". The cover of *Ark Angel Manifesto* encapsulates the world that we live in today.

Are you living through a storm in your life? Do you feel like you can barely keep your head above the water, as the waves of life crash over you? Maybe you want to be better prepared for that upcoming storm that you know is approaching! What we all want is hope, peace, and deliverance from the turbulent world we live in today.

The Author, Rob Klassen, has mastered these navigational skills in *Ark Angel Manifesto*! Rob Klassen is a seasoned minister, teacher, and counselor. Rob is gifted in these three areas as well as the gift of writing. Rob has an incredible ability to bring clarity and wisdom to the personal circumstances we daily face in our lives. In fact, you can call him ***"Your Clarity Adviser"!*** Rob is gifted with the ability to help you see clearly through life's turbulent storms!

Rob's desire for you through writing this book is to equip you with the tools to not only survive the turbulent world we live in today but to triumph! By putting into practice the teachings of *Ark Angel Manifesto*, you will become world-changing conquers! You will rise above the stormy seas full of faith hope and perseverance! *Ark Angel Manifesto* not only gives us Life-jackets but sea charts and a speedboat as well!

Follow Rob Klassen as he brings fresh eyes and teachings to the epic event of Noah and the Ark. What better place to start then in the foundational book of the Bible, Geneses! Study the life of Noah and how it directly applies to your life today! *Ark Angel Manifesto* will have you walking and working side by side Noah as he builds the ark. You will feel his struggles and experience the joy-filled adrenalin of overcoming adversity! You will witness how culture and media affect your ability to successfully overcome your adversity. Rob will have you discovering the deeper meaning of the rainbow and how it applies to you! You'll discover why you would want to be an Ark Angel.

You will:

Learn how to be an ark builder for this generation!

Learn how to provide protection, provision, deliverance, and victory for your family, community, and country.

I know you will be in good hands and sound teaching with Rob as your guide! I have known Rob for many years and can attest to that. Rob has passed through those stormy turbulent seas and arrived at the rainbow on the other side! My heart leaped for joy when Rob put pen to paper so he could pass his life manifesto to all of us who read this book.

Warren Barker

Travelling Philosopher and Friend

Introduction

Do you ever get that sinking feeling? You know, that feeling when it seems that no matter what you do, you feel like you are drowning? Or you feel suffocated? Maybe you feel like you don't fit in. It could be that you are wondering when you will see results for all your efforts. Maybe you feel all alone even when there are people all around you. Life can be like that. Life doesn't always fit into our preconceived plans. Turbulence and turmoil indicate that adjustments are required. All through history, adjustments have been the pathway to GREATNESS!

Let's take Daniel and his three friends, or Joseph, or David. What about the Apostle Paul or Moses? We could also include Esther and Ruth as well. All these people had to adjust to strange and difficult situations.

When you look at your life - what situations created the need for serious adjustments?

- A disease,
- A divorce,
- A death of a loved one,
- A career move,
- A dream from God,
- A divine revelation,
- Being fired, or
- Relocating to a new country.

How well did you do? I have to admit that I have had many opportunities to make adjustments. Let me recount a few:

ARK Angel Manifesto

I lived in 18 houses by the time I was 18 years old and went to 10 different schools by the time I graduated from High school. Talk about adjustments!

When I was 13, I grew six inches in six months. I felt really awkward and needed to adjust.

When I was sixteen, I preached my first sermon and it was at the Union Gospel Mission. While preaching, an individual got up, started walking towards me and threatening me. It was difficult to concentrate on preaching my well-prepared sermon. I had to adjust. When I was nineteen, I was volunteering at a Christian Drop-in Center in the inner city. One evening, a man came in and said to us, ***"If you are here again next week, I will come here and kill you!"***

I decided to go back to the drop-in center the next week. I have to be honest, I did make an adjustment to my prayer life, my attitude and priorities.

After 17 years of marriage, my wife at the time left me and took our children. I've never seen them since and that was over 12 years ago. My whole life changed in a moment!

Major adjustments were required! I needed to adjust my theology, my faith, my dreams, my career, and my future!

What's your story? What detours were thrust in front of your path?

How did your adjustments work out?

There is a man in the Bible who faced uncertainty. He teaches us a lot about life, detours, and destiny. He reminds Christians and the Church of many principles required so we DO NOT SINK! His name is Noah!

And this book is, ***ARK Angel Manifesto!*** I invite you to build the ARK that will stay afloat and arrive safely on the other side.

ARK Angel Manifesto

This book will reveal principles that are required building materials for the ARK so you will have safe sailing and bring many others with you!

I truly believe that you will be able to relate to the information within this book. I also believe that as you read, there will be a quickening in your spirit. I believe that the intersection of the information and your spirit is where *REVELATION KNOWLEDGE* will release transformational power in your life!

May your reading turn into REVELATION!

Meet you on the other side!

Rob Klassen

Rational knowledge comes from the mind through reason and study. True knowledge comes from the heart, through meditation and revelation by the Holy Spirit.

Mark Virkler

PART ONE
NOAH - The Original ARK Angel

ARK Angel Manifesto

ARK Angel Manifesto

I believe that there is a connection between Noah and the present day Christian! We would benefit from exploring Noah as we equip ourselves for the future. By looking into Noah's life, I believe the relevance is applicable to every believer today!

This book is not a book explaining the end times. This is not a book analyzing the science behind the FLOOD. This is not a doctrinal treatise on eschatology.

This is a message for today. It is a message for every believer who desires to be a light in darkness; to walk in their divine destiny; to be a guide to the lost; and the believer who is willing to count the cost to live in intimate communion with their Savior.

The name of the LORD is a strong tower; the righteous run to it and are safe

---

Proverbs 18:10

A good name is to be chosen rather than great riches, loving favor rather than silver and gold.

Proverbs 22:1

ARK Angel Manifesto

Chapter One

The Name

I had the privilege of naming three children. Names are important to me.

The middle name of my first born daughter is ***Chayil.*** It has a variety of meanings but all are ***significant.*** It means the following:

Woman of Valor

Virtuous

Strength, might, efficiency, wealth, army

CHAYIL Glory is the manifested power and glory of the Lord Jesus Christ *in* and *through* His servants. "At that time they will see the Son of Man coming in a cloud with **power** and **great** glory." Luke 21:27. The Hebrew word for power and great glory is **CHAYIL**. The prophet Isaiah and Jesus talk about times when darkness increases in the world to a level of potential devastation that triggers a move of God to save and restore the world.

Therefore, CHAYIL Glory is an outpouring of God's glory (awesome majesty) manifesting in love, hope, mercy, goodness, power, and salvation. It will flow in and through His believers (You), resulting in changed lives and transformed communities.

CHAYIL Pillars are worship, wisdom, power, honor, favor, wealth, and influence.

I encapsulated the meaning of Chayil into ***"SUCCESS body, soul and spirit"*** as so aptly described in Proverbs 31. This was my BLESSING for my firstborn!

My second born was named Serena Cherith. I captured the meaning by BLESSING Serena Cherith with ***"I can sing the Song of Peace because God keeps His Promises!"*** Serena means "song of peace" and Cherith represents God keeping His promises. The word Cherith literally means "to cut". In their culture, they would cut a covenant also known as a Blood Covenant.

The description of "cutting a covenant"

In those days, contracts were made by the sacrificial cutting of animals, with the split carcasses of the animals lying on the ground. Then both parties to the covenant walked through the animal parts together, repeating the terms of the covenant. The Lord made a covenant in Genesis 15:18 which literally meant, "The Lord cut a covenant."

God showed this was a unilateral covenant. Abram never signed the covenant, but rather passively watched while God signed it for both of them in the ritual.

Therefore, the certainty of the covenant God made with Abram is based on the foundation of the character, integrity, and ability of God! It was based solely on the IDENTITY of God, not on who Abram is or what Abram would or could do. This covenant could not fail because God cannot fail. "

Paul Ziegler explains the **Blood Covenant Ceremony** like this:

"In ancient times the blood covenant was common among almost all of the people of the Middle East. It was a way of establishing a binding contract between two men. What we call the Old and New Testaments could easily be called the Old and New Covenants. The typical blood covenant contained nine parts or steps.

These steps are as follows,

1) The two people exchange coats or robes. To a Hebrew, the coat or robe represented the person himself; so when he offered the other person his robe, he was offering himself; even his very life itself.

2) They take off their belt and offer it to the other person. The belt, also called the girdle, was used to hold your sword, your knife, and other fighting instruments. In this way, you were saying to the other person that you were offering him your protection. If someone attacks you, they also have me to deal with. Your battles are my battles.

3) "CUT THE COVENANT". In this part, an animal is killed and cut down the middle and the two halves are laid opposite each other. The two parties to the covenant pass between the two halves of the animal and are saying, "May God do so to me and more if I break this covenant. This is a blood covenant, and cannot be broken.

4) Raise the right arm and cut the palm of the hand and clasp each other's hand and mingle your blood. This is saying to the other person, "We are becoming one with each other. To intermingle the blood is to intermingle the very life of both people.

5) Exchange names. Each one takes part of the others name and incorporates it into their own.

6) Make a scar or some identifying mark. The scar was the outward evidence of the covenant that others could see and know that the covenant was made. Sometimes they would rub the cut in the hand to make the scar, then anyone who wanted to fight you would know that he not only had to fight you but another as well.

7) Give terms of the covenant. Both parties to the covenant stand before a witness and list all of their assets and liabilities because each one takes all of these upon himself. You are saying, "Everything I have is yours and everything you have is mine. If something happens to you, your covenant partner will see to it that your wife and children are taken care of.

8) Eat the memorial meal. A loaf of bread is broken in half. Each feeds his half to the other saying, "This is my body, and I am now giving it to you." Then they take wine as a symbol of his blood and says, "This is my blood which is now your blood."

9) Plant a memorial tree. The two then plant a tree as a memorial to the covenant and sprinkle it with the blood of the animal that was killed for the covenant offering.

These nine steps do not have to take place in the same order that they are listed here. "**The Blood Covenant**, Paul Ziegler

Now as we discover from Genesis 15, Abram believed that both he and God were going to make the covenant together because that is how it was done.

But God caused a deep sleep to come upon Abram and as he was waking up, he saw God walk through the divided animals by Himself making the covenant binding ONLY by Him!

When a person went through the severed animals, they are declaring that if they break the covenant, they a decreeing that what was done to the animals or worse will be done to them.

God knew that Abram could not keep the terms of the covenant so God entered the covenant and made it binding **only** upon Himself.

Therefore, God promised to provide, protect and promote Abram and his descendants.

Now Cherith (to cut) was the brook where Elijah was sent by God in order for God to Protect, Provide and then Promote Elijah to a new level of Power & Authority! See 1 Kings 17-18.

Therefore, I blessed Serena Cherith ***"I can sing the Song of Peace and Confidence because God has cut a blood covenant with me to Protect, Provide and Promote me! I sing songs of JOY because God keeps His PROMISES!"***

My third born was named Joseph Elliot. I BLESSED him with ***"Jehovah is GOD who will use you to INCREASE His purposes, empower you to EXCEL as an ambassador of God's Kingdom and through it give you (Multiplication)* increase in every area of Life! You will be a voice of truth and evangelism. "**

Joseph in Hebrew means "to add, to increase, to add on top of something already achieved (in other words to EXCEL or Multiply). And Eliot means, "My God is the Lord!" or "My God is Jehovah!" or "God has helped – empowered, equipped & elevated"

One dictionary described the name Joseph this way:

"A complicated, emotional guy who genuinely wants the best for everyone around him. (Sounds like the Joseph in Genesis, doesn't it?) He is incredibly kind, intelligent, passionate and funny. He makes an exceptional **best friend** and will be an **amazing** husband/father. "

He is extremely **loyal**. We could look back into Genesis and see this loyal characteristic in Joseph. He was loyal to Potiphar even if it meant going to jail. He was intelligent and had the favor of God on his life as demonstrated in the massive **INCREASE** produced when he was working for Potiphar and when he was promoted to second in command over the nation of Egypt. We see his **compassion** for the general population and the **intelligence** to plan ahead in order to provide for the nation and surrounding nations during a famine. We even see his **kindness** when making provision for his brothers who had betrayed him. He was **loyal** even to those who had been disloyal to him.

So I BLESSED my son with Joseph Eliot, ***"Jehovah is GOD who will use you to INCREASE His purposes, empower you to EXCEL as an ambassador of God's Kingdom and through it give you (Multiplication)*** **increase in every area of Life! You will be a voice of truth and evangelism. "**

****

Well, the name Noah also has a significant meaning. Noah means "**rest, repose, peace or comfort**". No matter what was going on around him and the changes in society, he seemed to possess inner rest enabling him to hear the voice of the LORD and see the society around him through the eyes and heart of God.

This is the account of Noah and his family. Noah was a righteous (right living, just) man, the only blameless person living on earth at the time, and he walked in close fellowship with God. Gen. 6:9 NLT

Why did Lamech, give Noah this name? It seems that Lamech's desire for his son was for him to be a leader of his generation - from toil to peace, from cursed to blessed and to reverse the curse and open the door for his generation to find true rest. Even though Lamech lived a life of violent unrest, it seems that he wanted something better for his son.

BIG Egos have little EARS!

Dr. Robert Schuller

Chapter Two

The Culture

There once was an advertising exec who lived his whole life without ever taking advantage of any of the people he dealt with. He was honorable and well respected. In fact, he made sure that every account he worked on was a win-win situation.

One day, while walking down the street, he was tragically hit by a bus, and he died. His soul arrived up in heaven, where he was met at the Pearly Gates by St. Peter himself.

"Welcome to Heaven," said St. Peter. "Before you get settled in, though, it seems we have a problem. You see, strangely enough, we've never once had an advertising exec make it this far, and we're not really sure what to do with you."

"No problem, just let me in. " said the ad exec.

"Well, I'd like to, but I have higher orders. What we're going to do is let you have a day in Hell and a day in Heaven, and then you can choose whichever one you want to spend eternity in"

"Actually, I think I've made up my mind . . . I prefer to stay in Heaven."

"Sorry, we have rules…"

And with that St. Peter put the ad exec in an elevator, and it went down-down-down to hell. The doors opened and the ad exec found himself stepping out onto the putting green of a beautiful golf course. In the distance was a country club, and standing in front of him were all his friends - fellow ad execs that he had worked with and they were all dressed in tuxedos and cheering for him. They ran up and slapped him on his back, and they talked about old times. They played an excellent round of golf and at night went to the country club, where he enjoyed an excellent steak and lobster dinner. He met the Devil, who was actually a really nice guy and he had a great time telling jokes and dancing. The ad exec was having such a good time that before he knew it, it was time to leave. Everybody shook his hand and waved goodbye as he got on the elevator.

The elevator went up-up-up and opened back up at the Pearly Gates, and St. Peter was waiting for him.

"Now it's time to spend a day in heaven." So the ad exec spent the next 24 hours lounging around on clouds and playing the harp and singing. He had a great time, and before he knew it, his 24 hours were up and St. Peter came and got him.

"So, you've spent a day in hell, and you've spent a day in heaven. Now you must choose your eternity. "

The ad exec paused for a second and then replied, "Well, I never thought I'd say this, I mean, Heaven has been really great and all, but I think I had a better time in Hell."

So St. Peter escorted him to the elevator and again the ad exec went down-down-down back to Hell. When the doors of the elevator opened, he found himself standing in a desolate wasteland covered in garbage and filth. He saw that his friends were dressed in rags and were picking up the garbage and putting it in sacks.

The Devil came up to him and put his arm around him. "I don't understand," stammered the ad exec. "Yesterday I was here and there were a golf course and a country club, and we ate lobster, and we danced and had a great time. Now all there is here is a wasteland of garbage, and all my friends look miserable. "

The Devil looked at him and smiled.

"That's because yesterday you were a prospect, today you're a client."

This fictitious story shows us the power of culture.

Culture is . . .

"Our behavioral patterns, belief systems, principles, and ways of living are derivatives of our culture.

Culture is the invisible bond which ties people together. It refers to the pattern of human activity. Our cultural values and beliefs manifest themselves through our lifestyle. Our moral values represent our culture. The importance of culture lies in its close association with the ways of thinking and living.

Culture affects perception, and perceptions drive behavior. Thus, the culture we belong to has a direct impact on our decisions, attitudes and lifestyle..

Group culture determines the behavioral norms of the group. To be accepted as part of the group, we tend to follow what the group decides for us. Influenced by the norms or rules laid out by our culture, we tend to act in accordance with them. Our culture defines people's expectations from us. In an attempt to fulfill them, we shape our behavior and personality to suit our culture. " Buzzle. com/articles/why-is-culture-important

During the time of Noah, there was only one culture. It was a pervasive culture that had evolved by slowly abandoning the truth. The world Noah was living in, was not conducive to the morals and values that God had planned for His people. The culture of God had been replaced by the culture of evil.

Noah was not one of those teenagers that was always telling his parents that "EVERYBODY is doing it!"

The Voice translation, explains the culture in Noah's times this way:

By Noah's time, nearly all people are drugged on the fumes of their egos. Wickedness has become the number one, all-consuming human addiction.

The Eternal One saw that wickedness was ***rampaging*** *throughout the earth and that evil had become the* ***first thought*** *on every mind, the* ***constant purpose*** *of every person.* At that point, *God's heart broke, and He regretted having ever made man* in the first place. *Gen. 6:5-7 The Voice (Italics mine)*

The LORD observed the extent of human wickedness on the earth, and he saw that ***everything*** *they thought or* ***imagined*** *was* ***consistently*** *and* ***totally evil****. So the LORD was sorry he had ever made them and put them on the earth.* ***It broke his heart****. Gen. 6:5-7* NLT *(emphasis mine)*

I understand this pain as do many parents. As parents, we have desires and dreams for our children. We want them to succeed and reflect our character, values, and beliefs. We want to protect them from the evil around them by teaching the truth about healthy relationships, morality, integrity, respect, their identity in Christ.

Yet our children have free will. They may reject our values, renounce our faith, and refuse our relationship advice. We see them abandoning the foundation of faith and righteousness we built for them.

The pain is immense! The pain is excruciating! The pain breaks our heart! We can see how their choices will destroy them yet we are not able to change their heart.

We still LOVE our children but because we see the destructive demonic force coming upon them, we sometimes wish they had never been born. We love them too much to see them self-destruct before our loving eyes!

I believe this is the heart attitude that God had!

▪ His love was not reciprocated.

▪ His values were not embraced.

▪ His beautiful purposes for them were rejected.

▪ His character was not respected.

▪ His righteousness was repudiated.

▪ He saw the pain they were causing.

▪ He saw the evil they were embracing

▪ He witnessed their rationalization of their rebellion.

▪ He knew where their actions and beliefs would destroy the world.

▪ He loved them too much to watch them self-destruct before His loving heart.

▪ So He wished they had never been born!

Then came Noah onto the scene!

Noah must have been a misfit!

He was right living in a wrong living world! He was in a close relationship with God while those around him were in a close relationship with their evil passions!

Noah was thinking about the heart of God while society was thinking about themselves.

Noah **receptive**, society rebellious.

Noah **holy**, society hedonistic.

Noah **personal peace**, society perverted pride.

I'm sure that he was bullied, mocked, disrespected and laughed at!

TIME to ask a few Questions

• *If Noah lived today in our technology culture and moral perspective, how would people respond to him?*

• *Do you think that he would be a victim of cyber-bullying?*

• *Do you think that he would be treated with respect or ridicule?*

• *If he lived where you live right now, why not describe how your community would treat a present-day Noah.*

• *Let's get a little bit closer – how would you treat a present-day Noah if they went to your school, employed where you work or even went to your Church?*

You will find peace not by trying to escape your problems, but by confronting them courageously. You will find peace not in denial, but in victory.

J. Donald Walters

Chapter Three

The Crisis

My Spidey senses are tingling!

Welcome to the world of Spiderman! His Spidey senses would locate criminal intent, prevent a crisis and catch the criminal in the act! If there was a crisis about to take place, Spiderman could sense it. He was a superhero who averted crisis and protected his community.

Noah was not Spiderman. He was much more than a fictional crime fighter!

Noah was committed to protecting his community from the ultimate crisis – a WORLDWIDE Flood! He dedicated his life to avert a cosmic crisis.

He was not a secretive crime fighter, he was a ***Preacher of Righteousness!***

There was a CRISIS between God's beautiful plans for society and their violent vile corrupt lifestyle! Something had to be done about the situation.

"They lived at a time when the world had become vile and corrupt. Violence was everywhere. God saw that **the earth was in ruins,** *and He knew why:* **all people on earth except Noah had lived corrupt lives and ruined God's plans for them.** *He had to do something. "Gen 6:11-12 (The VOICE)*

God had to do something and something radical because the rebellion was so radical! Society was violent and all they could think about was violent, vile and evil thoughts; and all they were doing was violent, vile and evil acts!

The solution was a **VIOLENT STORM**!

Chapter Four

The Action Plan for Deliverance

Action Heroes fight to deliver the world from disaster!

God gave Noah a plan for **deliverance** against **disaster**, **destruction** and **demonic domination!** It came in the form of blueprints for building an Ark!

Let's put this in context. The building of the ark must have taken around 100 years to complete. The actual time of the ark construction is debated. Now that is a BIG project. But there is more to the situation. No one knew what rain was. The Scripture that mentions no rain before the great flood is found in Genesis 2.

The Eternal God had not sent the rains to nourish the soil or anyone to tend it. In those days, a mist rose up from the ground to blanket the earth, and its vapors irrigated the land. (Genesis 2:5 - 6) The VOICE

OR

But a mist (fog, dew, and vapor) used to rise from the land and water the entire surface of the ground.

(Genesis 2:6) AMP

There are other factors to consider that lead one to believe there was no rain before The Flood. In the account of Noah described in the New Testament, it tells us that rain or anything like it, had never happened before. This was a NEW phenomenon!

It was by faith that ***Noah*** *built a large boat to save his family from the flood. He obeyed God, who warned him about things* ***that had never happened before****. Hebrews 11:7 NLT (Italics mine)*

Another factor to consider is the timing of the formation of rainbows which presents evidence that it did not rain on the earth until after the Flood.

Then God said, "I am giving you a sign of my covenant with you and with all living creatures, for all generations to come. I have placed my rainbow in the clouds. It is the sign of my covenant with you and with all the earth. When I send clouds over the earth, the rainbow will appear in the clouds, and I will remember my covenant with you and with all living creatures. Never again will the floodwaters destroy all life. When I see the rainbow in the clouds, I will remember the eternal covenant between God and every living creature on earth." Then God said to Noah, "Yes, this rainbow is the sign of the covenant I am confirming with all the creatures on earth." Genesis 9:12-17 NLT

Rainbows would not have existed before the Flood since they are created by the refraction of light passing through suspended water (water drops). It seems likely that God used the new phenomena known as rainbows to be a "reminder" to both Him and mankind of the promise made following The Flood.

Stanley Manahan, an environmental chemist explains it this way:

"The earth before the flood was a lush tropical forest with large amounts of vegetation. Before God caused the Flood, there would have been less wind and atmospheric turbulence. Winds are caused by temperature differences caused by the tilt of the earth's axis, mountain systems, and ice caps. All of these cause unequal regions of hot and cold on the globe which produce the various winds. The pre-flood earth was warmer, had more vegetation, had smaller oceans, and had smaller mountains compared to today.

The atmosphere of the earth, before the flood, had less particles for rain to condense around than what we find today. Particles called condensation nuclei are absolutely essential to the formation of rain drops.

"Some atmospheric particles . . . formed by the evaporation of water from droplets of sea spray, are natural and even beneficial atmospheric constituents. Very small particles called condensation nuclei serve as bodies for atmospheric water vapor to condense upon. "

(Manahan, Stanley E., *Environmental Chemistry* (7th edition).

Lewis Publishers - CRC Press. Washington DC. Page 267)

The lack of rain, however, did not mean the world before the flood was dry. Since the earth would have been warmer and laden with moisture that was not condensed, there would have been an extremely efficient condensation cycle.

This would mean the planet would have been watered, not by water drops falling from the sky, but by a very heavy mist or fog each day.

Science confirms the WORD!

Chapter Five

The Resilience of Faith in God's Word

Psychological resilience is defined as an individual's ability to successfully adapt to life tasks in the face of social disadvantage or highly adverse conditions. Noah possessed resilience!

He had a lot of adapting to do. Like building a solution to a problem that did not exist yet. Hearing a celestial being give him building instruction for a 100-year project. His behavior created a huge social disadvantage resulting in adverse conditions for himself and his family.

If it took him almost 100 years to build the ark and none of the people on earth had ever seen rain, his daily activity would have appeared RIDICULOUS!

Imagine Noah getting up in the morning, putting on his work clothes and beginning to build. Day after day; week after week; and month after month. I am sure his neighbors were curious, to say the least.

"Hey, Noah, what are you doing?"

"I'm building an ark."

"What's an ark?"

"Well, an ark is a huge boat, specially designed to withstand intense storms and violent rainfall!"

"Who needs something like that?" "I mean, what is a storm and rain anyway?"

"Rain is large drops of water falling from the sky and a storm is those drops of water being blown violently by wind, blinding us and even though we have never seen rain or storms for that matter, they are coming."

"What has caused you to have such crazy ideas and stupid imaginations?"

"God told me all this!" The neighbors laugh.

They mocked him and ridiculed him! Maybe they would sing ***"Rain Drops Keep Falling on my Head"*** whenever they would walk by his construction site.

This reminds me of a powerful story located in NY City.

There were two people walking down busy Fifth Avenue. One person was a prominent businessman; the other was a Native American in NY for a conference. They were walking and talking together when suddenly the Native American stopped and said

"Did you hear that cricket?"

The business-man replied, "How in the world could anyone hear the sound of a cricket with all this traffic noise and hustle and bustle?"

Immediately, the Native American walked slowly, turned a corner and picked up the cricket that was making the "noise".

Astonished, the business-man exclaimed, "How did you do that?" The Native American said, "I will demonstrate." He reached into his pocket pulled out a few coins and dropped them on the sidewalk – suddenly numerous people around them STOPPED and began looking around for the money.

The Native American declared

"It's not people's hearing ability but what they value that DETERMINES what they hear!"

Noah heard the Voice of God, the others didn't!

Because of this,

Noah kept building and the people around him kept laughing!

Day after day and month after month, Noah maintained his story, his activity, and his resolve even though there was NO VISIBLE EVIDENCE! He had heard the Word of God!

His ark building was an act of Preparation for Salvation and Proclamation of Warning!

Imagine doing something that everyone else didn't believe in.

Not only did they not believe in your vision and actions; they ridiculed you, belittled you and bombarded you with their negativity.

Yet you continued to build. That's **RESILIENCE**!

But Noah was more than resilient. He had influence with his family.

When God decided to initiate a rescue plan for humanity, He ONLY found Noah! No ONE ELSE!

Genesis 6 describes to us a perverted, evil and totally ungodly world.

They lived and believed everything that was OPPOSITE to the values and character of God!

They were not reflecting God's image as they were created to do.

So God was going to eliminate them all. Then He found ONE PERSON, Noah who was righteous and in close relationship with Him.

Thus the rescue mission began.

"Noah was a **righteous** man, the **only blameless person** living on earth at the time, and he walked in close fellowship with God." Genesis 6:8 NLT Emphasis mine

This also means that Noah's wife and children were NOT RIGHTEOUS when Noah began building the ark but they were WHEN they entered the ark!

How do we know this? Well, in Ezekiel 14, when the Israelite nation was wandering away from God and His values, Ezekiel under the inspiration of the Holy Spirit declared the following.

> *"Or suppose I were to pour out my fury by sending an epidemic into the land, and the disease killed people and animals alike. As surely as I live, says the Sovereign* LORD, *even if* **Noah**, *Daniel, and Job were there,* ***they wouldn't be able to save their own sons or daughters. They alone would be saved by their righteousness.*** Ex. 14:19-20

So while Noah was building the ark, and as people watched, ridiculed and mocked Noah, his family were also watching Noah. Noah probably had his sons help with the building, yet at this time they did not believe in what their father was doing. As time went along, they must have seen something in their father that made them realize the truth of his beliefs and vision. They must have entered into a relationship with God also. Then these men must have had great influence on their wives so they also entered into a relationship with God and separated themselves from the culture of depravity all around them.

Remember Noah's righteousness could only save himself (Ezekiel 14:14, 20) so the others that gained entrance on the ark (Noah's family members) . . .

Must have joined him in his faith sometime between Noah being the only righteous person on the face of the earth and the entrance into the ark just prior to the flood.

Noah had many brothers and sisters as confirmed in Genesis 5:30 "After the birth of Noah, Lamech lived another 595 years, and he had other sons and daughters

Yet not one of them joined him in the ark because none of them shared his faith. They embraced the predominant culture of evil and depravity. In 595 years, just imagine how many sons and daughters Lamech could have fathered!

Just imagine a family gathering! Noah's brothers and sisters discussing his building project and mocking the absolute insanity of it.

Sitting around the table eating when all of a sudden one of his brothers asks, "Brother Noah, so what are you going to eat while you are trapped in this big boat?" "Are you going to take your fishing rod so you can catch a fish or two?" "Why do something so stupid, when you can feast with us? Just look at this spread!"

Yet with all this family dynamics, Noah's wife and children followed His faith and not the attitude and beliefs of their cousins, uncles, and aunts.

Noah must have had quite the character of integrity for his wife and children to be so attracted to it that they were willing to abandon the prevailing culture for the UNKNOWN!

Not only was Noah an Ark Builder with perseverance and undaunted commitment, he was also a Preacher of Righteousness! 2 Peter 2:5

A **preacher** is a spokesperson of spiritual truth and a revealer of the heart of God. **Righteousness** is the level of a right, whole and pure relationship with God!

Noah was a Preacher of Righteousness, therefore, he was a spokesperson of spiritual truth and the heart of God pointing people to the restoration of a relationship with God through faith! ***I believe that Noah was encouraging his family, friends, and community to join him in the ark.***

John Gill, in chapter 22 of the *Pirke R. Eliezer*, quotes Noah's words according to Jewish tradition:

> ***"Be ye turned from your evil ways and works, lest the waters of the flood come upon you, and cut off all the seed of the children of men."***

Tradition shows Noah giving both a warning and a means of salvation. If this extra-biblical source has any truth in it, then Noah is asking for people to repent, which would certainly fit with his own source of salvation. Noah was not saved because of his righteousness—at least not in a worldly, human effort sense. *Hebrews 11* tells us from where Noah's righteousness came. The Greek word is *dikaiosune* (δικαιοσύνη), which refers to a form of righteousness that is **UNATTAINABLE** by law or by merit.

Hebrews 11:7 says, "By **faith** Noah, being divinely warned of things not yet seen, moved with godly fear, prepared an ark for the saving of his household, by which he condemned the world and became heir of the righteousness which is **according to faith**. "

This level of righteousness is acquired ONLY by Faith!

Noah's salvation, like ours, was by **grace**. He could not do anything to attain righteousness for himself.

So his faith, first of all, was demonstrated in his obedience to God's Word in a situation he had never experienced, or could never humanly perceive. A WORLD WIDE FLOOD!

Secondly, his faith not only showed up in his obedience but it showed up in his preaching.

We could say it this way, he ***obeyed God's Word and he announced God's agenda.***

We can, therefore, say that Noah was the first evangelist mentioned in the Bible.

Christians have gleaned many valuable lessons from Noah and the ark. But one fact is often overlooked. He was the first evangelist mentioned in the Bible. Are there any lessons his life can teach us about how to present the gospel? Absolutely!

For one, Noah faced the same circumstances that Christians face today.

Just as most people today do not believe Jesus is coming back at all, let alone soon, the people of Noah's day did not know when the Flood was going to happen. Like I said earlier. *Noah was thinking about the heart of God while society was thinking about themselves.* Equally if we are intent on thinking about the heart of God, we'll be at odds with and confusing to a world just thinking about themselves.

However, they people of Noah's time, were informed that there was indeed going to be a Flood. This information came from many sources:

1. From the fact that Noah was actually building an Ark.

2. From the warning of God's Spirit (Genesis 6:3 says, "And the Lord said, 'My Spirit shall not strive with man forever, for he is indeed flesh; yet his days shall be one hundred and twenty years. '")

3. From the words of Noah himself.

Secondly, like people today, almost certainly the people of Noah's day were busy enjoying the pleasures of life and did not believe or care that judgment was coming.

We know that there was a lot of room remaining in the ark due to the calculations of biblical mathematicians. Therefore, there was room for many more people to enter the ark! **All they had to do was repent and turn to God!**

In the same way, salvation is available to "whoever calls on the name of the Lord" (Romans 10:13, NKJV). Notice that the eight occupants of the Ark entered by a door—and there was only one door— which was not closed by Noah, but by God— "the Lord shut him in" (Genesis 7:16, NKJV). *Jesus said, "I am the door. If anyone enters by Me, he will be saved"* (John 10:9, NKJV).

This also means that ENTERING through the door of religion, the door of a denomination, the door of a Church building, the door of culture, the door of tradition, the door of following a spiritual leader WILL NOT bring anyone salvation! Those doors will only lead to deception, disappointment, discouragement and ultimately disaster.

When we think about Noah, culture, and the character of God; the FLOOD account teaches two KEY truths about the attitude of God toward us.

1. He is angry with sin and will punish it one day.
2. He loves us and sends us a way of salvation if we will only repent and turn to Him.

With all the opposition that Noah faced, he is a living testimony of Faith, Consistency, and Resilience! The Church of the 21st Century can learn much from his testimony!

Chapter Six

Results

Where there is action, there are results!

Where God's instructions are followed, there are RADICAL divine RESULTS!

First occurrence of Pitch POWER

One of the results of obeying the instructions of God was pitch POWER! What do I mean by pitch POWER?

Here are some of the instructions:

Genesis 6:14

Make yourself an ark of gopher wood;
make rooms in the ark, and cover it inside
and outside with pitch. – NKJV

Now, we are very familiar with the first part of the instructions but what about the second part of the instructions?

"And cover it inside and out with pitch."

Some translations refer to this as tar. One translation just calls this an instruction to waterproof the ark. I would like to suggest a far deeper meaning of this instruction.

The Hebrew word for pitch is ***Kafar.***

Here is a Jewish translation of this verse. ***JPS Tanakh 1917***

Make thee an ark of gopher wood; with rooms shalt thou make the ark, and shalt ***pitch*** *it within and without with* ***pitch****. (Emphasis mine)*

Now this instruction could not be done until the ark is completed. Therefore, the meaning of pitch is intensified. WHY?

Noah is just applying a water sealant on the ark, so what is so significant about that. Everyone knows you have to do that. So why is this instruction located in a place of emphasis within the building instructions?

Because the Hebrew word for "pitch" is **PACKED WITH MEANING**! Tim Hegg explains it very well in the following excerpt:

"In general, the scholarly work on this verb has given rise to three suggested root meanings:

(1) To cover,

(2) To ransom,

(3) To wipe away.

Obviously, these suggested meanings have some overlap.

We may expand the idea of these three as follows:

1. To cover = to hide the sin or transgressions from the sight of the deity in order to avert his anger.

2. To ransom = to make some kind of payment to the deity for the transgression in order to appease His anger.

3. To wipe away = to expunge the transgression and to restore the status of sanctum (holiness) whether to an individual, a group, a holy object, or a holy place/region. We see, then, that the meaning of kafar as "to wipe away,"

The translation, "wash away" is well represented by the words that convey "pardon," "to be propitious toward someone," and "to forgive."

The Meaning of כפר Kafar "To Make Atonement" by Tim Hegg

Strong's Concordance defines the word Kafar this way: A primitive root; to cover (specifically with bitumen); figuratively, to expiate or condone, to placate or cancel -- appease, make (an atonement, cleanse, disannul, forgive, be merciful, pacify, pardon, purge (away), put off, (make) reconcile(-liation).

"If this is the case, then the base meaning is "to wipe away," for in these contexts כפר has a direct effect on sancta—it "wipes" sancta "clean," meaning it restores the status of sanctum (holiness) to that which had been defiled. In this way, the "qal" meaning of the verb, "to cover with pitch" is connected to the meaning of the piel, "to wipe (with blood)." – Tim Begg

---

One could say that God instructed Noah to smear or cover the ark with reconciliation and forgiveness both inside and outside.

The Jubilee 2000 Translation captures this.

"Make thee an ark of cedar trees; rooms shalt thou make in the ark and shalt reconcile it within and without covering it over with pitch." (Heb. ransom or atonement)

One could also say, this instruction was to **place a protective coating of righteousness on the ark so that JUDGE-MENT could not penetrate anything living inside the ark!**

OR, Noah was instructed to smear the ark inside and outside, in order to hide the sin or transgressions from the sight of the God in order to avert his Judgement.

The ark was covered in RIGHTEOUSNESS so that the Law of Righteousness could not affect those inside the ark.

The Law of Righteousness demands judgment and punishment! Kafar protects from the impact of the Law of Righteousness!

Now, I know that many people believe that the pitch was there to waterproof the ark. I have difficulty with that interpretation.

Let's look again at Genesis 7:11-12

"On the 17th day of the 2nd month in Noah's 600th year, ***ALL*** *of the subterranean waters erupted from the depths of the earth and burst sky-ward, covering the land. The casements of the heavens cracked open,* [12] *dousing heavy rains over the watery earth for 40 days and 40 nights. "* *The Voice*

"**ALL** the underground waters erupted from the earth, and the rain fell in mighty **TORRENTS** from the sky." *NLT*

I don't know about you but I am thinking about our modern shipbuilding technology and the storms that have caused them to capsize and sink. Now, these storms have had torrents of rain but they do not have the ALL encompassing components of the Noah Flood.

Just imagine cypress or gopher wood held together with a tar seal-ant staying afloat when ALL the subterranean water ERUPTING and VIOLENTLY SURGING upward to the sky PLUS Tor-rential rains pulsating the ark from above!

In the natural, I do not believe that the ark could stay afloat in such conditions and I do not believe that our modern day ships could survive this storm, either! Our ships have sunk in far lesser conditions.

Therefore, I believe that there is a supernatural significance to Kafar!

GRACE!

The covering of Righteousness, Atonement, and Holiness is what kept the ark afloat! ***Judgement could not touch the ark!***

It was COVERED in GRACE!

Now that is the Power of Pitch!

That is the Power of Following Divine Instructions!

That is the Power of Obedience!

That is the Power of a Personal Relationship with God! ***That is the Power of GRACE!***

Radical Results of Righteousness

Noah heard from God. He was the only one righteous in the whole world. Not even his family were on board! Yet after many years, his wife, sons and their wives entered the covenant promise with Noah.

So what happened next?

Chapter Seven

New Residence – The Ultimate Relocation

Relocation, the process of vacating a fixed residence in favor of another. A move like this comes with a lot of apprehensions. (I understand relocation! Remember that I lived 18 in houses by the time I was 18 years old and attended 10 different schools!)

Noah was about to get relocated – ***not to a new city, not to a new country but to a new world!***

The Ark was packed and ready to float. Now what?

First, Noah finished building the ark and he entered the ark.

Then the Lord said to Noah, "Come into the ark, you and all your household, because I have seen that you are righteous before Me in this generation.
Genesis 7:1 NKJV

Second, his immediate family entered the ark. Many times, those closest to us refuse to follow our vision and call from God.

I know many pastors admired by many people and yet whose children did not follow their faith but instead they rebelled!

Sometimes those who see us from a distance are more eager to follow us than those closest to us. Those closest to us can clearly see our faults, failings and character flaws.

Noah must have possessed a consistent character of integrity, love and compassion for his children to follow his bizarre, never heard of, vision and behavior. His family entered the ark in contrast to Noah's brothers and sisters who preferred the ***CULTURE OF COMPROMISE***.

Third, they brought "seed" for the NEW WORLD! The seed was living things. They were so convinced of the Word of God that they brought animals and birds to repopulate the NEW WORLD.

"You shall take with you seven each of every clean animal, a male and his female; two each of animals that are unclean, a male and his female; also seven each of birds of the air, male and female, to keep the species alive on the face of all the earth." **Genesis 7:2-3**

No survivors! No people, no animals and no birds! It must have been a very tearful journey to the ark, KNOWING not one of their friends or family would survive. This would be the last time seeing them, sharing activities with them – laughing, eating, celebrating and doing business with them.

They must have been certain that they had heard from God!

They were saying GOOD-BYE to EVERYTHING they knew!

It takes GREAT Faith to enter the UNKNOWN but that is what Noah and his family did! The majority chose the known, the comfort zone, and the predictable. They thought they were **playing it safe**. HOW WRONG THEY WERE!

Human nature hasn't changed very much since the Days of Noah!

Fourth, the TEST of FAITH! God reveals His plan to them and He tells them that they get to wait for seven days when nothing will happen. Everything will appear just the same as before they entered the ark.

I wonder what their friends and relatives were doing during those seven days. I think they might have called out to Noah saying he made a HUGE mistake; he hadn't heard from God like he claimed; he had wasted 100 years of his life on foolishness and that he even deceived his own family with his foolishness.

I believe that the door wasn't shut for those seven days. They had an opportunity to abandon ship and return to their culture.

Also, I believe that the door was open for others to join Noah in the ark!

All they needed to do was repent of their sins, renounce their Culture of Corruption & Compromise, and re-assert their Relationship with God!

This was the Suspenseful Seven!

Day One – they remained in the ark.

Day Two – they remained in the ark

Day Three – with a total lack of visible evidence of a flood and the voices of unbelief reverberating in their ears and heart, **they remained in the ark.**

Day Four – the flood waters were NOT RISING but the opportunity for DOUBT and abandon ship was rising!

Day Five – What if this is all one BIG mistake? What if I have been deluded all these years? What if our friends, cousins, uncles, and aunts are right? What if the flood never comes? We will be the perennial JOKE of the world! We will NEVER be able to live down our delusion and self-righteousness! What will be our defense on the eighth day? **Yet they remained in the ark!**

Day Six – Mixed feelings Anticipation and Excitement on the one hand; Dread and Doubt on the other! Like the song***, "Should I stay or should I go?"*** Maybe they were practicing their speech if the flood didn't come or maybe they encouraged each other in the Word of God which Noah had heard. I believe it was the second option that they chose! **They remained in the ark!**

Day Seven – Doubt was DEFEATED! God's Word was embraced and **they remained in the ark!**

✦ If you did not know the end of the story.

✦ If you were one of the sons or wives.

✦ If you were sitting there in the barn of unsettled animals.

✦ If you were hearing the mockery of unbelief outside with no corresponding evidence of your decision

✦ Would you have remained in the ark?

✦ If you were on the outside looking in, would you have joined Noah in the Ark?

Like I mentioned before, I believe that those seven days, people could have joined Noah and family if they would BELIEVE the WORD of GOD that Noah had shared with them. But none believed!

- Peer pressure was too strong!
- Being accepted was too attractive!
- Status quo was too enticing!
- Their lifestyle was too intoxicating!
- Their habits too binding!
- Their fear of rejection too powerful!
- **And they remained in the world!**

Fifth, God shut the door!

"Then the LORD closed the door behind them."

This is a symbol of salvation. We can obey God, follow His instructions but if the door remains open, we WILL DROWN!

We CANNOT be in the doorway – a half in the Ark (Covenant Promises of God) and a half in the world system – Culture of Corruption. That would keep the door open and we would be destroyed!

Even IF the door is ***mostly*** closed, the flood waters would still rush in and engulf us!

Water is attracted to cracks and openings! The water here represents the values and culture of the world's belief system. It doesn't need a WIDE OPEN chasm to sink a ship, it merely needs a crack, a crevice, small entry point in order to seep in and sink the vessel.

Also, the world does not need a wide open chasm within a person to sink a LIFE. It only needs a small entry point!

What small entry points do you have in your LIFE which creates an environment making you VULNERABLE to causing your Destiny to DROWN?

Sixth, God's Word was proven RIGHT!

"On the 17th day of the 2nd month in Noah's 600th year, all of the subterranean waters erupted from the depths of the earth and burst skyward, covering the land. The casements of the heavens cracked open, dousing heavy rains over the watery earth for 40 days and 40 nights. " Gen. 7:11-12 (Voice)

Water SUDDENLY EXPLODED from EVERY direction!

"When Noah was 600 years old, on the seventeenth day of the second month, all the underground waters erupted from the earth, and the rain fell in mighty torrents from the sky." Genesis 7:11 NLT

These were NO gentle showers of blessing!

This was a violent storm, an EXPLOSIVE reality! It was as violent as the people were violent and evil!

They were receiving what they had sown!

"Those who sow seeds into their flesh will only harvest destruction from their sinful nature. But those who sow seeds into the Spirit shall harvest everlasting life from the Spirit. " Gal. 6:8 Voice

---

OR

"If you plant in the field of your natural desires, from it you will gather the harvest of death; if you plant in the field of the Spirit, from the Spirit you will gather the harvest of eternal life." Gal. 6:8 GNT

The Amplified Translation explains it very clearly when it says:

"For the one who sows to his flesh [his sinful capacity, his worldliness, his disgraceful impulses] will reap from the flesh ruin and destruction, but the one who sows to the Spirit will from the Spirit reap eternal life. " Gal. 6:8

Those who chose to remain outside the ark, because their fleshly desires were too strong and their spiritual connection to God and His covenant promises non-existent, reaped a harvest of destruction and death!

Faith consists in believing when it is beyond the power of reason to believe.

Voltaire

Because with every action, comment, conversation, we have the choice to invite Heaven or Hell to Earth.

Rob Bell

Chapter Eight

Reflections on Spiritual Decisions

In **REFLECTION**, we are able to peel away the opaque film that hinders clear perception of TRUTH. Reflection, when properly activated, can elevate one's understanding and also create awareness of insights otherwise hidden from our cluttered thoughts. Reflection can also bring to the surface deep personal meanings called ***Revelation Knowledge***!

Have you ever felt like circumstances were coming at you like a FLOOD? You are bombarded with life's circumstances and you are beginning to go under.

You may have even cursed yourself by saying, ***"I can't win for losing"***.

Just like the people of Noah's time, an umbrella isn't going to save them. Drift wood isn't going to save them.

There is a book entitled, ***Dig Your Well before You Are Thirsty*** by Harvey Mackay. The premise of this book is that IF you wait until you are thirsty, you will not have the energy, time or resources to dig the well before you dehydrate and die.

We could have titled this book, ***Build Your Ark Before It Floods.***

If it took Noah nearly 100 years to build the ark with God's specific instructions; the people in Noah's day will not have the time or knowledge or energy to build a boat to withstand the deluge the moment of a FLASH FLOOD (especially when it was the Kaphar –Righteousness - that kept it afloat and in one piece not human technology)!

The WORD of GOD gives us instructions on how to build an ark so the flood waters of circumstances will not swallow us up! What are the FLOOD waters rising up against you?

- Sickness
- Debt
- Relationships
- Unemployment
- Emotional and Mental struggles
- Confusion
- Addictions

I am reminded of Isaiah 54:17.

"But in that coming day no weapon turned against you will succeed. You will silence every voice raised up to accuse you. These benefits are enjoyed by the servants of the Lord; their vindication will come from me. I, the Lord, have spoken!" Is. 54:17

One could say,

"NO FLOOD WATERS directed at you will SINK YOU!"

Those with Noah found "rest" from the storm just as Noah's father had hoped except he desired that this "***rest"*** would be for all people and not just Noah and his family.

Remember that the name Noah means ***rest, peace and safety***.

This reminds me of a story of Alexander the Great.

There was this soldier in Alexander the Great's army. He was a young soldier. One day during a battle, he ran from the battle and went AWOL!

He was caught and brought to Alexander the Great for sentencing. The usual punishment was DEATH! Alexander the Great was in an exceptionally good mood that day and after a severe scolding, he let the young soldier go. As the young soldier was leaving, Alexander the Great commanded that he stop!

"Young man, what is your name?"

The young man almost collapsed under the ominous weight of fear. With panic filled eyes, he s-t-u-t-t-e-r-e-d

"M-m-m-y n-a-m-e is Aaaalexaaaannderrr"

Immediately, Alexander the Great EXPLODED and yelled at the young soldier . . . .

"Change your ways or change your name!"

Noah didn't have to change his ways because he was already in a right relationship with God. And he didn't have to change his name because he was ***resting*** in the instructions and promises of God!

(Remember that was the meaning of his name – Rest.)

Let's review the results of Noah's obedience and the impact of the Flood.

The Flood totally changed the entire landscape of the earth!

The geography was dramatically changed with huge mountains and valleys formed by the immense hydraulic pressure of the flood waters.

- The climate totally changed.
- Anthropology changed because the life expectancy after the flood seriously decreased.
- Sociology changed because the entire social framework was dismantled and a new society began.

ACTUALLY, EVERYTHING CHANGED!

The canopy covering the earth was broken and destroyed. The greenhouse environment was replaced with seasons, rain, drought, lakes, rivers, oceans and of course – the **Rainbow**!

Chapter Nine

Rainbow- The Covenant of Relationship

The Rainbow is a majestic symbol of God's Promises, His Love and His commitment to His creation. But before we look deeper into the Rainbow, let's set the stage of what happened between the Flood and the Rainbow.

Between the time that the door of the Ark was closed and sealed from the outside by God until Noah and family were reunited with terra firma, we're talking a span of one year! That is a LONG time to be cooped up in a huge wooden box tossed to and fro with numerous (I mean, NUMEROUS) animals!

Hey kids, have you ever complained about your chores? Imagine being Noah's kids on an ark with a GIGANTIC Zoo to manage!

So what does the Bible tells us about this time?

On the 17th day of the 2nd month in Noah's 600th year, all of the subterranean waters erupted from the depths of the earth and burst skyward, covering the land. The casements of the heavens cracked open, dousing heavy rains over the watery earth for 40 days and 40 nights. Gen 7:11-12

After the seven day wait in the ark with absolutely nothing happening **– no signs, no clues, no warning** – **SUDDENLY** something happened. We are not just talking rain. These were no showers of blessing!

As a matter of fact, the sudden deluge was not the rain at all. It was the ENTIRE underground water supply trapped inside the earth that erupted like a volcano all over the earth.

This catapulted the ark upward like one of those amusement park rides, but this was NO AMUSEMENT! Then the rain began to attack the earth from above. **"And the rain fell in mighty torrents from the sky." Genesis 7:11b NLT**

We are talking an Ark Sandwich with deluge as the two slices of "**torrent bread**"! Again, we are not talking scenic cruise to our favorite vacation destination!

From NOTHING to Nautical Nastiness in a moment of "SUDDENLY"!

I wonder what thoughts, words, screams and actions filled the ark by Noah and his family. What were your thoughts, words, screams when you went on your first CRAZY ride!

No one will ever know their thoughts, words and screams because God sealed the ark so no TMZ, paparazzi photographer, and no National Inquirer could get the inside scoop.

This was the SUDDENLY and then came the 40 days and 40 nights of constant torrential rain! I don't think food was on their minds. I don't even think that they thought about those who rejected the ark. I think the wild torrential adrenalin pumping ride distracted them.

You may say that what I am imagining is not in the Bible. You may be right. Please let me explain.

A number of years ago, I was privileged to go on a Mediterranean cruise. We entered turbulent waters on our way to France. The waves were reaching the third level of the ship and we were tossed about like ragdolls. I was leaning heavily on a support pillar. I have to admit, I wasn't thinking about the other people because I was too busy hanging on. Talk about Intentional Living! I am fairly confident that the storm Noah faced was significantly more severe than my experience.

My ship and storm experience lasted only several hours; theirs lasted 40 days and 40 nights or more! I invite you to imagine what was going through their minds, and **imagine what emotions were cascading over their souls.**

"But God remembered Noah and all of the wild and domesticated animals with him in the ark. When it was time, God sent the **wind** *to blow over all of the earth, and the waters began to subside. The subterranean waters from the depths of the earth and the casements of the heavens were again closed. The drenching rains that once fell from above finally stopped. All of the waters gradually receded from the land. At last, after* ***150 days,*** *the waters abated; and on the 17th day of the 7th*

month, the ark at last came to rest on the mountains of Ararat.
"Genesis 8

In the above verses of Scripture, I underlined some keywords that would demonstrate the unsettling storm like conditions did not end after 40 days and 40 nights. God caused a wind to rise up. We all know what wind combined with water creates! It creates a storm with massive waves! So even after the subterranean waters and the torrential rain had stopped, the massive amount of water was still being churned up by the wind. Yes, the winds were instrumental in causing the waters to evaporate but in the meantime Noah, his family and the animals were experiencing turbulence beyond our imagination.

I'm sure we all have heard of or even watched TV programs or newscasts where storm watchers are involved. They have all kinds of advanced technology for monitoring, predicting, and recording these storms. They would catch a glimpse of the storm before it actually arrived. Their technology enabled them to predict when and where and what degree of severity the storm would be. What the storm watchers are doing is quite dangerous and precautions are paramount. Also the storm watchers through their scientific data could predict the length of the storm.

Noah had none of this!

He'd never seen a storm before; had no clue about it severity. He did not have computer and satellite technology to prepare for the storm through calculations and visual observations. And he had no idea how long the storm would last or how long he'd be trapped in that floating prison.

When you add this total lack of knowledge and uncertainty of duration into the equation, please try to imagine their emotional state during this time bobbing up and down in the water. No shoreline to be seen. No signs of life to be seen outside the ark.

Let's put it this way. Imagine you are in an elevator and it suddenly stops in-between floors. The doors cannot be opened. You call for help but it seems like no one heard you. You wait, and wait and wait. For hours, you wait in darkness, fear and uncertainty!

What are your thoughts, emotions, words and behavior? I thought so! Now MULTIPLY that experience by 40 days and 40 nights knowing that there is no one outside to help because they have all drowned! Now add another 150 days of fierce winds.

Welcome to the experience of the Righteous Eight!

We have an advantage because we can read Genesis 5 all the way to the end of Genesis 8 in about 10-15 minutes. It doesn't take us very long to discover the conclusion to their wild adventure.

It is like those one-hour crime shows on TV. They discover the problem, they are confused as to what to do, they create a strategy, they solve a crime and finally they still have time to debrief - all before the hour is up.

Noah did not have this luxury and yet we know his faith was much more stable than the erratic motion of the waves against the ark!

Now that is FAITH!

As I meditate on this passage of Scripture and try to put myself into the hearts, minds and emotions of Noah and his family, I am challenged by how easily I get discouraged and frustrated when I have had to face adversity. My faith is more like the raging waves up and down and up and down than the stability of Noah's confidence and conviction in the Voice of God.

How about you?

What is your natural tendency when faced with adversity – is it excitement and anticipation of what the mighty hand of God is about to do or is it despair, frustration and a deflated confidence as the circumstances suck the life out of you?

I think the default emotion for most of us would be the latter but I believe the first reaction could be ours as we get to clearly know the love, compassion, and power of our God.

So how do we get to know this love, compassion and power?

Firstly, through the studying of the Word of God not as an academic text but rather as a portrait of the character of God.

Secondly, through meditation on the Word of God.

Thirdly, by allowing the Holy Spirit to teach, guide, and comfort us as a supernatural bridge to the revelation of the ***Gracious Loving Magnanimous Favor-Filled Focus*** of the Heavenly Father for his children!

Let us fast-forward to after the water had abated and dry land emerged. Their stomachs have settled; the ark had landed; and they were about to open the door to a brand new world!

They knew it would be nothing like the world they left behind. They did not know what to expect when the door would open.

One thing I do know is that the only people on the planet were those about to walk out of the ark. What a difference from having family, relatives, friends, playmates and colleagues to interact with.

Can you imagine leaving behind everything that you know and everything that you have, to be dropped into an unknown location with no training and no understanding of what you're walking into? I'm sure that is how Noah and his family were feeling. They had been on the ark for such a long time that the closed quarters, the erratic bobbing up and down by the waves, the smell of the animals and the darkness of the covered ark had become normal for them.

Remember, they had been in that ark for almost a year. Now the door to the unknown is again about to open. When they walked into that door before the flood, they were walking into the unknown and now that same door when opened will again cause them to walk into the unknown.

"But God was not finished. He had more to say to both Noah and his sons.

Eternal One: Look, for I am now going to make a pact, a special covenant, with you and all your descendants. This covenant also extends to every living creature in the world—the birds, the domesticated animals, and every wild animal on the earth—as many as emerged with you from the ark. As part of this covenant, I promise you I will never again wipe out all living flesh by means of flooding waters.

Never again will a flood destroy the earth. As a sign of this perpetual covenant I now make between Me and you and all living creatures along with you, as well as all future generations, I will hang a rainbow among the clouds. It will serve as a sign of the covenant between Me and the earth. And from now on, whenever a cloud rises over the earth and a rainbow appears in the sky,I will remember My covenant—My promise I have made between Me and you and all living creatures. No waters will ever again turn into a flood powerful enough to destroy all living creatures. When that rainbow appears in the clouds, I will see it and remember this eternal covenant I have made with all living creatures.

Look for the rainbow, and remember My promise. With it I sign the covenant I have made between Me and all the living creatures residing on the earth.

"Gen. 9:8-17 Voice

I really like how the Amplified Version expresses the character of God and his promises.

"When I bring clouds over the earth, that the rainbow shall be seen in the clouds, and I will [compassionately] remember My covenant, which is between Me and you and every living creature of all flesh" Genesis 9:15 AMP

God's not going to just remember the eternal covenant of promise when he sees a rainbow but rather he is going to **compassionately** remember his covenant.

He wants this new world to experience abundance, prosperity, fruitfulness and most of all, a dynamic personal relationship with their God who loves them and has great plans for humanity.

Now when you see a rainbow after a rain shower, what do you think?

- Do you reflect on its beauty?
- Does it remind you of God's covenant to you about no more global flood?
- Does it remind you of the beautiful protective fruit of righteousness?
- Do you see the rainbow as God's powerful promise and plan for a better world?

Why do you think the rainbow is so colorful and so beautiful? It could have been a black band in the sky.

OR

It could've been one big **red circle** with a slash through it like we see on labels all around us like no smoking or no swimming signs. That would be a great reminder on the covenant. You know a big red circle with a slash through it and a bunch of waves in the middle.

So why so colorful? I know we can give scientific answers to that question but I believe there is a deeper and more beautiful meaning.

I believe that God does not want them to be reminded of the trauma in the PAST but rather the beautiful possibilities of the FUTURE!

- It's beautiful because God's PLANS for them are beautiful.
- It's beautiful because God's PROTECTION over them is beautiful.
- It's beautiful because God's PROVISION for them is beautiful.
- It's beautiful because God's PERSONAL RELATIONSHIP with them is beautiful.

- Also, why is the symbol of the covenant not a picture, not a banner, not a sign, or not a document? Why is it in the form of arc?

I believe again that there are several reasons for this:

• Both the beginning and the end are uncertain, just like the uncertainty they had entering the ark and then the uncertainty when exiting the ark.

• The rainbow's arc is in a similar form of the canopy over the earth before the flood. Remember how before the flood there was no rain and yet all the plants flourished because of the canopy that God had created as a dome of protection and productivity.

• The rainbow shape has the reflection of royalty and with it combined with the clouds can often look like a crown. This points to the sovereignty of God and that when he promises a promise it comes with a GUARANTEE.

• The rainbow is in the shape of what we now use to protect us from rain – the umbrella! It's a symbol of protection and comfort and shelter in the face of a storm. Just as the umbrella protects us from the face of a storm, the rainbow is God's promise to protect everyone who has a covenant relationship with Him.

• The rainbow is in the shape of an **arc** and God's divine protection of those in a covenant relationship with them was an **ark**. This is interesting and I believe it means that the arc shape of the rainbow is a **continuation** of God's **Covenant Promise** to **PROTECT** and **PROVIDE** for everyone who enters a covenant relationship with Him.

• The rainbow shape is kind of like a colorful ribbon or banner. It actually reminds me of a song I sang as a teenager when I was a camp counselor. Here are the lyrics to that camp song:

> The Lord is mine and I am His,
> His banner over me is Love. 3X
> His banner over me is Love!
> He brought me to the banqueting table,
> His banner over me is Love. 3X
> His banner over me is Love!
> He lifted me up to heavenly places,
> His banner over me is Love. 3X

His banner over me is Love!
He is the Vine and we are the branches,
His banner over me is Love. 3X
His banner over me is Love!
Jesus is the rock of my salvation,
His banner over me is Love. 3X
His banner over me is Love!
There is one way to peace through the POWER of the Cross
His banner over me is Love. 3X
His banner over me is Love!

And since the rainbow is like a banner that represents the covenant of love with God, I think I should add another verse to this camp song:

The rainbow in the sky is a Promise of God's Love
His banner over me is Love. 2X
The rainbow in the sky is a Covenant of God's Love
His banner over me is Love.
Yes, God's banner over me is Love!

We have now looked at the story of Noah catching a glimpse of the punishment, protection, provision and promises of God for humanity.

There is more to the story of Noah that we could examine in detail. Maybe at another time or in another book, I will do just that. But for now, let's take the nuggets that we have learned from the life of Noah and begin to apply them to our lives, to our communities, to our churches, to our countries, and to our world!

Remember what the name Noah means? Let me remind you – Noah means ***rest***, it means **peace** and it means **stability/safety**.

Now the question for you as you continue to read this book is – ***how can you bring rest, peace, and stability to your world?*** How can you become an effective messenger of ***Hope, Peace and Deliverance in a Turbulent World?***

There is but one Church in which men find salvation, just as outside the ark of Noah it was not possible for anyone to be saved.

Thomas Aquinas

Part TWO
The NEED for ARK Angels Today

A system of morality which is based on relative emotional values is a mere illusion, a thoroughly vulgar conception which has nothing sound in it and nothing true

---

Socrates

Aim above morality. Be not simply good, be good for something.

Henry David Thoreau

Chapter Ten

Just for Comparison Sake

"For the coming of the Son of Man (the Messiah) will be just like the days of Noah." Matthew 24:37 (VOICE)

If we spent any time watching the news, we can clearly see that the culture of our time is resembling the culture of the pre-flood era more and more closely!

When Jesus described the events that will surround His second coming, He said, ***"Just as it was in the days of Noah, so will it be in the days of the Son of Man. They were eating and drinking and marrying and being given in marriage, until the day when Noah entered the ark, and the flood came and destroyed them all"*** (Luke 17:26–27).

Jesus was pointing out that, although the people of Noah's day were totally depraved, they were not the least bit concerned about it. They were carrying on the events of their lives without a single thought of the judgment of God.

Noah is described as "a preacher of righteousness" (2 Peter 2:5), meaning he had spent years warning his family, friends and neighbors what the Holy God was about to do.

NO ONE LISTENED!

The depravity and ungodly lifestyles of the entire world at that time were enough to cause the Lord to "regret that He had made man" (Genesis 6:6).**Many scholars believe that part of the need to destroy every human being except Noah and his family was because of the sin mentioned in Genesis 6:1–4! The sin of when "the Nephilim were on the earth in those days, and also afterward, when the sons of God.**

This phrase has been interpreted as a reference to:

(a) Royalty or rulers possessed by fallen angels,

(b) The descendants of Seth who called upon the Lord (see 4:26), or

(c) Fallen angels (cf Job 1:6) would have sex with the humans' daughters, the women bore them children who became mighty warriors. "

As evil reproduced and overtook the world, the most merciful act God could perform was to start over!

It is interesting that God allowed Noah nearly one hundred years to complete the building of the ark. Through all that time, God patiently waited (1 Peter 3:20). Scripture seems to imply that Noah Preached to the people of that time about what was coming (Hebrews 11:7).

They did not believe Noah and were content with their wickedness and idolatry.

Their hearts were hard and their ears dull.

No one repented, and no one cared to seek God.

Jesus said that the world will be much the same before He returns to set up His earthly kingdom (Matthew 25:31–33).

He warned us to "be ready, because the Son of Man will come at an hour when you do not expect him." Just like in the times of Noah, the people didn't take the values and purposes of God seriously.

Second Timothy 3:1–4 gives us a clear picture of the state of the world before Jesus comes and most likely also describes the world in the days of Noah.

That passage says,

"But mark this:

There will be terrible times in the last days. People will be ***lovers of themselves, lovers of money****, boastful, proud, abusive, disobedient to their parents, ungrateful, unholy,* ***without love****, unforgiving, slanderous, without self-control, brutal,* ***not lovers of the good****, treacherous, rash, conceited,* ***lovers of pleasure rather than lovers of God.*** *"*

It is becoming increasingly obvious that, to understand what the world was like in the days of Noah, we only need to watch the evening news!

Just a few questions for you to answer before you continue

1. What values and ideas do the news, movies, ET, TMZ, magazines promote?

2. What values, priorities, and behavior do they present as normal, exciting, desirable, and to be imitated in order to fit in?

3. What attitudes do they encourage us to adopt and openly express?

4. Does this list look familiar?

Lovers of themselves (vanity) (believe they are ENTITLED to have their desires met IMMEDIATELY; and believe they are the center of the universe and MUST be treated with admiration and respect while they treat others in a manner of manipulation, rudeness, demanding and cruelty) (other people's feelings, worth, needs, talents are totally discounted) (they demand compliments, adulation, people fussing over them, and very often reverence)

1. Lovers of money (self-indulging GREED), status seeking, using the power of money to control others, and so they can parade around looking like the rich and famous even when their hearts and soul are impoverished.
2. Boastful,

3. Proud,
4. Abusive,
5. **Disobedient to their parents**,
6. Ungrateful (complaining),
7. Unholy,
8. **Without love** (sex as a biological act of hormones rather than an expression of love, loyalty and unity), **"Without love**" is expressed and demonstrated in a variety of ways such as promiscuity, different partners, different genders, rough sex, sex as a game of playing with other people's emotions, to get a promotion at work, S&M, role-play, rape, fantasy, and kinky sex are just a few examples of making life an experiment rather than an expression of proper love for oneself, proper love for others and a sincere love for God)

- Unforgiving (grudges, revenge and back stabbing gossip),
- Slanderous (lie in order to destroy people),
- Without self-control (feelings and emotions determine behavior) & (they worship at the altar of their feelings, hormones and desires) eg. ***"If it FEELS good, do it!",***
- Brutal (mean, malicious, excessive meanness, rage fueled violence and totally destructive in nature),
- Not lovers of the good (or attracted to evil, edgy, repulsive and immoral activities) ,
- Treacherous,
- Rash (impulsive),
- Conceited,
- **Lovers of pleasure rather than lovers of God**

Here is an interactive awareness project designed so you can capture the message of the following chapters.

Can you guess that Media?

In the left column, you'll see the characteristics of the culture before Christ returns. The next three columns are the three main medium that reflects the present day cultural values, priorities and lifestyles. Your job is to think of titles of movies, TV shows, magazines that promote the characteristic in the left column. You can definitely put more than one title in each box.

It might be fun to even make this a competition between a few people to see who can create the most complete list in 15 minutes. After the 15 minutes, you can compare notes and discuss the differences and similarities of the charts and what thoughts came to your mind and in your heart after completing this assignment.

Characteristic	Movies	TV Shows	Magazines
Lovers of self			
Lovers of Money			
Boastful, Proud & Abusive			
Disobedient to Parents			

Sexuality without Love			
Ungrateful & Complaining			
Unforgiveness & Revenge			
Lack of Self-Control			
Brutal Violence			
Attracted to Evil and Immoral Activities			
Treachery			
Impulsive			
Conceited & Arrogant			
Passion for Pleasure but No Passion for God			

Let's compare the times of Noah with the times we are living in now. In the far right column place a checkmark for each of the characteristics and activities clearly evident in our culture.

Days of Noah Genesis 6: 4-7	Culture of Judgement Described Matthew 24:37 37 As it was at the time of Noah, so it will be with the coming of the Son of Man.	Our Present Day Culture
Now at that time and for some time to come, a great warrior race lived on the earth. Whenever the sons of God would have sex with the humans' daughters, the women bore them children *who became mighty warriors.* In the days of old, they became famous heroes, *the kind people tell stories about!*	Romans 1:18 ff Voice 18 For the wrath of God is breaking through from heaven, opposing all *manifestations of* ungodliness and wickedness by the people who do wrong to keep God's truth in check. 19 These people are not ignorant about what can be known of God, because He has shown it to them *with great clarity.* 20 From the beginning, creation in its magnificence enlightens us to His nature. Creation itself makes His undying power and divine identity clear, even though they are invisible; and it voids the excuses *and ignorant claims* of these people 21 because, despite the fact that they knew the one true God, they have **failed** to show the ***love,*** **honor**, and **appreciation** due to the One who created them!	

By Noah's time nearly all people are drugged on the fumes of their egos. Wickedness has become the number one, all consuming human addiction.

[5] The Eter-
nal One saw that
wicked ness was
rampaging
throughout the
earth and that evil
had become the
first thought on
every mind, the
constant purpose
of every person. [6-
7] *At that point*
God's heart
broke, and He re-
gretted having
ever made man *in
the first place.*

Do you know anyone who takes all the credit for their success and never even think of given credit to God for providing everything they need for the success they have experienced?

Instead, their lives are **consumed** by ***vain thoughts that poison their foolish hearts***.

Many people are consumed by many things in their lives. Some are consumed with money; some are consumed with relationships; some are consumed with sports; some are consumed with movies and entertainment; and some are consumed with fantasies. This verse tells us that many people are consumed with vain thoughts; purposeless thoughts; meaningless thoughts and thoughts that have no positive return.

This could include negative thoughts; this could include pessimism and doubt; this could include bitterness and revenge; and this could include envy and jealousy. Instead of thinking on the goodness of God and his precious promises they choose to rather think about problems, negativity and things that poison their spirit

The New Testament gives more details. We will continue comparing the following New Testament descriptions with the characteristics and activities clearly evident in our culture.

I will give a running commentary of the characteristics described in the New Testament and their relevance to our present times. There is also a column to the right for your comments and personal observations.

You may believe that you are living in an ***ADVANCED Society*** when the trust is that the similarities to the past are striking!

On the next page you will see a descriptive chart of societal similarities with the depravity of the past.

[22] They **claim** to be wise;

These people have a lot of ***information*** *and they* ***believe that possessing information make one wise.*** *This is not true. We are living at a time in history when the volume of knowledge doubles every 18 months or less. But when you look at the world around you, are you seeing wisdom and character and virtue increasing at the same rate?*

I didn't think so. And therefore we can conclude that information and knowledge does not translate into wisdom.

But these people claim to be wise in order not to be accountable to the truth.

These individuals claim to be wise as a smokescreen for pride and an unwillingness to submit to a greater one.

It is actually arrogance not humility; it is resistance not responsibility; it is self-centeredness not servanthood; and it is a form of narcissism not an expression of love.

Doesn't this describe the world you live in?

Does this describe your community, your society and possibly even your heart?

But they have been exposed as fools, *frauds, and con artists—*
[23] ***only a FOOL would trade the splendor and beauty of the immortal God to worship images of the common man or woman, bird or reptile, or the next beast that tromps along.***

We live in the era of stock markets, NASDAQ, New York Stock Exchange and we live in a time where trading is at an all-time high. We know the basic principle is to buy low and sell high. If a person bought high and sold low, we would consider that a foolish trade and a foolish thing to do.

Who would trade a gold mine in full production for an acre of swampland? Not very many people unless they are delusional, insane, or extremely ignorant.

The people described in this passage are foolish traders. They are willing to TRADE

- The splendor,
- The beauty,
- The love,
- The promises of God, and
- Eternity for an image made out of wood or metal or plastic.

Do you know people who have made that trade as well?

You know the type, the people who expend so much energy keeping up with the Joneses, accumulating things and status, or trying to fulfill their desires and fantasies without acknowledging God?

[24] So God gave them just what their lustful hearts desired. *As a result,* they **violated** their bodies and **invited** shame into their lives.

God is the God of respect.

He will lead but he will not force people to live a wholesome, virtuous and fulfilling life.

Some people just insist on doing things their own way. So God will give them over to their choices and the natural consequences that are part of that.

The people described here, are very active in violating their bodies and inviting shame into their lives. You know the joking about colleagues who were caught walking the "*walk of shame*" that is often discussed over the watercooler.

So how do people violate their bodies? This could include self-harm –injuring themselves either as an expression of self-hatred or even an expression of Satanic ritual or sexual pleasure. But it needn't be physical in nature.

It could be using one's body in ways that the creator never created it for. Just a few verses later, he describes an example of violating their bodies. They chose sexual counterfeits – sexual encounters and relationships that do not reflect the character, values nor the design of God. These activities are described as unnatural, shameful and the results of carnal passions and depraved thoughts.

Does any of this describe the world you are living in?

---

[25] *How?* **By choosing a foolish lie over God's truth.** They gave their lives and devotion to the creature rather than to the Creator Himself, who is blessed forever and ever. Amen. [26-27] This is why God released them to their own vile pursuits, *and this is what happened*: **they chose sexual counterfeits—women had sexual relations with other women and men committed unnatural, shameful acts because they burned with lust for other men. This sin was rife, and they suffered painful consequences.**

[28] Since they had no mind to recognize God, He turned them loose to follow the unseemly designs of their depraved minds and to do things that should not be done. [29] Their days are **filled**

(Their days are filled, this reflects where their priorities and focus lie. If you ever watch the news or movies or entertainment shows they would not be difficult for you to find evidence of these things described in verse 29 as either being celebrated or sensationalized.)

With all sorts of **godless living, wicked schemes, greed, hatred, endless desire for more,** murder, violence, deceit, and spitefulness. And, *as if that were not enough,* they are gossiping, [30] **slanderous, God-**

hating, rude, **egotistical**, smug ***people who are always coming up with even more dreadful ways to treat one another.***

People are using their CREATIVITY to treat people in dreadful ways instead of using their creativity to elevate, encourage, and truly love others!

What if they used their creativity to treat other as created in the very image of GOD?

They don't listen to their parents; [31] **they lack understanding *and character.*** They are simple-minded, covenant-breaking, heartless, and unmerciful; *they are not to be trusted.* [32] Despite the fact that they are fully aware that God's law says this way of life deserves death, **they fail to stop. And *worse*—they applaud others on this destructive path.**

What is receiving APPLAUSE in your world that goes DIRECTLY against God's Loving Will?

The New Living Translation describes it this way:

[18] But God shows his anger from heaven against all sinful, wicked people who **suppress the truth** by their wickedness.

Have you witnessed media, politicians, corporations, etc. suppressing the Truth?

What comes to your mind?

[19] They know the truth about God because he has made it obvious to them. [20] For ever since the world was created, people have seen the earth and sky. Through everything God made, they can clearly see his invisible qualities—his eternal power and divine nature. So they have no excuse for not knowing God.

[21] Yes, they knew God, but they wouldn't worship him as God or even give him thanks. And they began to think up foolish ideas of what God was like.

As a result, their minds became dark and confused. [22]
Claiming to be wise, they instead became utter fools.

[23] And instead of worshiping the glorious, ever-living God, they worshiped idols made to look like mere people and birds and animals and reptiles.

[24] So God abandoned them to do whatever shameful things their hearts desired. As a result, **they did vile and degrading things with each other's bodies.**

Are there any examples of this in your present day culture?

[25] They **traded the truth about God for a lie.**

What evidence do you have of your culture trading the TRUTH about God for a LIE?

So they worshiped and served the things God created instead of the Creator himself, who is worthy of eternal praise! Amen. [26] That is why God abandoned them to their shameful desires. Even the women turned against the natural way to have sex and **instead indulged in sex with each other**.

[27] And the men, instead of having normal sexual relations with women, **burned with lust for each other. Men did shameful things with other men**, and as a result of this sin, they suffered within themselves the penalty they deserved.

Has your culture actively moved these lifestyle decisions from CONCEALED to CELEBRATED?

[28] Since **they thought it foolish to acknowledge God**, he abandoned them to their foolish thinking and let them do things that should never be done. [29] Their lives became **full of every kind of wickedness, sin, greed, hate, envy**, murder, quarreling, deception, **malicious behavior, and gossip.** [30]

Does this ring a bell when you think about the culture you live in?

They are backstabbers, **HATERS OF GOD**, insolent, proud, and boastful. **They INVENT new ways of sinning,**

In what ways have you seen this revealing itself in your world and culture?

And they disobey their parents. [31] They **REFUSE** to understand, **break their promises**, are **heartless**, and have **no mercy.** [32]

Give some examples of this in your world of experiences.

They know God's justice requires that those who do these things deserve to die, yet they do them anyway. Worse yet, they **encourage others to do them, too.**

In what ways do you see people actually encouraging others to sin in increasingly more vile ways?

So how many did you circle and check?

How many did you see in yourself?

I saw more in myself than I would like to admit.

They understood the times and had much understanding of what Israel should do.

---

1 Chronicles 12:32

Chapter Eleven

Democratization of Righteousness

We are living in a world that is becoming more democratic or at least that are the claims. This is not merely in the political realm but in every facet of life.

We're living in a time when morality, lifestyle and right & wrong are determined by a vote. We have come to the place where it is no longer **morality rules** but rather **majority rules**. We have voted on same-sex marriage; we have voted on abortion; we have voted on multi gender washrooms; we have voted on the legal possession of marijuana; we have even voted on our involvement in sex trafficking, sweatshops, and pornography.

The Irony of Democratic Morality:

• We have Catholic politicians voting for the abortion bill in order to retain their political power.

• We have had Jewish leaders whose relatives suffered in internment camps and many died in the Holocaust and yet they support the Holocaust of the unborn child.

• We have evangelical preachers involved in extramarital affairs and yet justifying it.

• We have Churches refusing to speak out against moral issues (that are actually in their Statement of Faith) by claiming that it is just too controversial.

• We have news networks that pan their video of an event to support their political and ideological beliefs rather than the objective truths.

• We have huge technology companies buying conflict minerals from the Congo so they can present a better profit margin to their stockholders. And as a matter of fact they will even fund Congolese child soldiers to protect their investments.

• We have politicians who get kickbacks and line their pockets by providing protection for illegal organizations that are destroying the country these politicians claim to represent.

• We have many Churches that have, under the guise of being culturally relevant, reduced Jesus Christ to ideology instead of the one true Savior.

• Preachers and priests who preach against premarital sexual activity and yet will bless those they know are living that lifestyle so they don't lose members in their Church.

• We are so concerned about offending other people that we, as representatives of the Lord Jesus Christ, are willing to offend God instead. What is wrong with this picture?

Now let us glance back to the days of Noah. Eight people entered the ark. We know that Noah was the eldest child and had many brothers and sisters younger than him. We also know that they had children. This is only one family group but there were many, many families like this on the earth.

Now if morality was determined by the Democratic vote, there would have been **no flood** and there would have been **no judgment**.

Sexual perversions would've been voted as legal and ethical.

Also Noah's beliefs and behaviors would've been voted unacceptable and possibly even criminal.

They may have voted in a gopher-wood tax or a counsel to approve an ark building permit.

The animal rights groups could vote against allowing animals of different species to be confined in a large wooden box together.

With a little bit of imagination, we could come up with a list of Democratic policies during the days of Noah that would have been enacted and totally changed this planet, if morality during the days of Noah was determined democratically

• Just imagine what your average day would look like: sexual lusts, lust for power, passion for control, subject to impulses and hormones, and a conscience that is seared and eyes blind to the truth.

Just imagine what you would look like.

Just imagine your emotional well-being or lack of well-being.

Just imagine your young children growing up in that culture of Democratic morality.

Like I said earlier only eight people entered the ark. That is definitely not a majority! Since Noah was called the Preacher of Righteousness, we know that he was inviting his friends, his family, and his neighbors to enter the ark with him. I'm sure he pleaded with them to forsake their culture of self-indulgence, embrace the truth of God and enter the ark.

And yet because of peer pressure, majority rules attitude and a total disregard for the principles and character of God himself, they chose to remain outside the ark.

There was no vote. There were no Council meetings. There was no flood referendum. There was no appeal process in the courts of **TRUTH**. There were no surveys to ascertain public opinion. So what was there?

Just as there is no vote or referendum or survey that can change the law of gravity, there also is no vote or referendum or survey that can change **The Law of Moral Truth**!

The universal ***Law of Righteousness*** took effect and the only one righteous was Noah.

Eventually his wife and children joined him in the ***Covenant of Righteousness.***

The universal ***Law of Righteousness*** was compelled to respond to the culture on the planet and it erupted with the same force that unrighteousness had erupted on the earth. And things changed.

So if we think that our opinions matter and the Democratic morality is a reality, we have forgotten the universal **Law of Righteousness**! And just like the law of gravity or the law of lift, the Law of Righteousness **MUST** respond in certain circumstances! It must respond because it is not subject to opinion or manipulation – it is a UNIVERSAL LAW!

Just imagine a person standing on the top of Sears Tower in Chicago, and decides to jump. And while he is in freefall, his opinion is that his mind can reverse the law of gravity! He believes that his wishful thinking, his words and his opinions could actually manipulate the law of gravity to keep him safe upon contact with the ground.

If you only had one word to describe that man's mindset what would it be?

I don't imagine that the word chose was the word **intelligent** or **wise** or a **ground breaker**! Well, maybe ground breaker in a different sense!

Whatever word you came up with to describe that man's actions, should be the same word you have in mind to describe a person who tries to DEFY the Law of Righteousness!

The Implications of Democratic "Righteousness"

1. A LIE becomes "true" if ENOUGH people vote for it.
2. Society tells God what to Believe.
   a. Here is a recent excerpt that reveals this agenda

Hillary Clinton said that Americans will have to change their religious convictions and cultural codes so they can pass laws. Convictions and belief systems of citizens should not stand in her way. Cultural codes and religious beliefs have to change, Hillary said.

She made these comments in April 2016, at the sixth annual Women in the World Summit. She's not only talking about foreign nations, her views are extreme and she wants those extreme views to dominate.

Americans have to change their beliefs because she says so? She will tell us what to think?

She was mostly referring to abortion but she can extend that to anything. She's now the thought police.

In addition, Tim Kaine who claims to be personally against abortion, agreed to repeal the Hyde Amendment in exchange for the VP position.

"The Hyde Amendment is a 1976 provision that bans the use of federal dollars for abortion services. The government under Clinton will force Americans to pay for abortion even if they see it as murder.

> *In a 2012 email that WikiLeaks says was sent to John Podesta, now chairman of the Clinton campaign, Voices for Progress president Sandy Newman writes that "there needs to be a Catholic Spring, in which Catholics themselves demand the end of a middle ages dictatorship and the beginning of a little democracy and respect for gender equality in the Catholic Church" and proposed that the Clinton team "plant the seeds of the revolution" to change Catholic teaching.*
>
> *Podesta replies, "We created Catholics in Alliance for the Common Good to organize for a moment like this.*
>
> *Likewise Catholics United. " He adds, "I'll discuss with Tara. Kathleen Kennedy Townsend is the other person to consult. "*
>
> *So members of the Clinton's inner circle created front groups to form a "Catholic Spring" — because, as their dear leader had announced, "Deep-seated cultural codes, religious beliefs and structural biases have to be changed"*
>
> Marc Thiessen writes a weekly column for The Post. He is a fellow at the American Enterprise Institute.

How about Canada? Well, below you will see a clip of how policy is seeking to tell Christians what to believe and how to behave.

https://youtu. be/2yC4Wj3b030

Just as Mrs. Clinton believes that Christians must change their beliefs, the present Prime Minister of Canada has this to say about Christians.

Justin Trudeau said: ***"Christians are the worst part of Canadian society"*** Canadian Times NEWS

Trudeau has also stated:

> "Trudeau told candidates in Canada's Liberal Party they can't run as pro-life, essentially banning those potential Liberal candidates (with strong pro-life religious convictions) from seeking office under the party banner.
>
> The National Post in Canada reported that Trudeau was simply "weeding out" pro-life candidates: *"It's not for any government to legislate what happens — what a woman chooses to do with her body, and that is the bottom line," declared Trudeau. "I have made it clear that future candidates need to be completely understanding that they will be expected to vote pro-choice on any bills."*
>
> *"That's part of the green-light process,"* he added. *"We check on a number of issues: How do you feel about the Charter of Rights and Freedoms, how do you feel about same-sex marriage, and how do you feel about pro-choice? What is your position on that?"*

The new policy allows for a pro-life incumbent in the party to remain pro-life, but it appears the left-wing party will no longer accept anti-abortion candidates.

"The Catholic Church in Canada has been critical of Trudeau's comments on abortion and for what they say is his inability to allow for Liberal Party members to exercise their conscience on abortion." The Christian Post

A group of Canadian Christian leaders is raising the alarm about what they say are attacks on their faith, citing barriers to a Christian university setting up a law school and doctors opposed to ending pregnancies being forced to refer patients elsewhere.

The group, including Charles McVety, president of the Institute for Canadian Values, pointed to a number of recent events they said equate to an attack on the Christian faith and impinge on Christians' ability to practice their faith.

The events include:

- A refusal by three provincial bar associations to accredit any potential law school graduate of Trinity Western University, which prohibits sexual intimacy outside heterosexual marriage among its students.

- A letter from Bank of Montreal to the Law Society of Upper Canada, which governs Ontario lawyers, arguing against accrediting Trinity Western's proposed law school.

- A commitment by the general counsel of 72 companies to promote diversity and inclusion.

• The College of Physicians and Surgeons of Ontario requiring that doctors with religious objections to birth control or abortion refer those patients to another physician.

> "Unfortunately, Christians in this country find themselves under attack," McVety said at a news conference on Parliament Hill.

• Doctors fight for their right to refuse care over religious beliefs

• Law society in Nova Scotia appealing ruling in favour of Trinity Western

• B.C. advanced education minister revokes approval for Trinity Western law school

"This is a violation, and we are calling on the Canadian government to stop this type of violation across this country."

British Columbia last December revoked approval for Trinity Western's proposed law school, which was planned to launch in 2016. Law societies in B. C., Ontario and Nova Scotia have voted to deny accreditation to future graduates.

But the Nova Scotia Supreme Court overturned the provincial law society's decision, which the Nova Scotia Barristers Society said yesterday it would appeal.

Trinity Western is also fighting the rejection of the Law Society of British Columbia and has said it will fight the rejection in Ontario too.

"We cannot be silent"

Law societies in Alberta, Saskatchewan, New Brunswick,

Prince Edward Island, Newfoundland and Labrador and Nunavut have decided to accept Trinity Western's graduates.

Lawyer André Schutten, who has intervened in a number of freedom of religion court cases, said regulations and laws "continue to be passed that restrict or curtail the religious freedom of Canadians."

"In various municipalities, Christians have been prevented or even fined for holding Church services in rented public space," said Schutten, legal counsel for the Association for Reformed Political Action.

"Professional bodies have indicated they want to force doctors to violate their consciences by either performing or being forced to refer for procedures that are immoral —including the horrific and barbarous act of killing innocent preborn children. "

Bill Prankard, president of the Bill Prankard Evangelistic Association, noted every Canadian is protected by the Charter of Rights and Freedoms.

"Enough is enough"

"While other groups are being granted more and more rights, we've been losing ours," Bill Prankard said.

"We are saying enough is enough. We cannot be silent anymore. "

Schutten said the group is looking for a statement from the federal government in support of religious freedom across the country, but admits the issues they raised Wednesday morning have more to do with provincial and municipal governments, as well as professional regulatory bodies. "[Such a statement] ready-sets the tone for inclusivity, tolerance of other world views, including the Judeo Christian world view," he said.

"Those levels of government also have to step up and be willing and ready to play fair with religious groups, including and especially I think Christian groups." CBC News

Now Trudeau has gone one step further. There are many Christian business people and tax payers in Canada. Many hire summer students. There is federal funding, available to subsidize these employment opportunities. Christians are about to be forced to choose between God and mammon!

Here is a headline that clearly reveals the direction Canada is headed.

Trudeau is asking religious Canadians to betray their conscience for federal funding

The Liberals have applied an ideological purity test to their applications for summer job grants

David Millard Haskell · for CBC News January 18, 2018

Here is an excerpt from the article:

Youth summer jobs

It sounds innocuous enough: Trudeau's Liberals have made changes to the youth summer jobs program, which provides grant money to various employers to hire students. The changes, announced in December, got little media attention until now.

Under the new rules, applicants must agree — by marking a box on an electronic form — that they respect charter rights, including "women's rights and women's reproductive rights." The office of the employment minister has said without the confirmation, an organization will not receive funding.

Their only "crime" is that their values don't align with those of our prime minister. It's ironic that Trudeau insists Canadians support "diversity and inclusion," when he himself does not.

I have given only a glimpse of the hidden or not so hidden agenda of ***North American political leaders who are TRYING TO TELL GOD WHAT TO BELIEVE***.

Let me add just one more recent agenda of ATTACK.

Here are a few excerpts from the article from Allen B. West:

Millionaire Gay Activist Declares War on Christians with 3 Awful Words 12:00PM EDT 7/26/2017 ALLEN B. WEST

"The megadonor bankrolling the LGBT movement and its allies in the Democratic Party says he will continue to "punish the wicked" who hold traditional views about sexual morality. Despite the legalization of gay marriage in all 50 states, tech millionaire Tim Gill said he is not satisfied with the movement's progress. He plans to use his immense wealth, corporate influence and political network to target red states with laws protecting religious people who disagree with the LGBT movement's worldview.

And you can clearly see in Mr. Gill's assertion that he intends to "punish the wicked."

LGBTQ activist Tim Gill wants to **"punish the wicked"** who oppose gay marriage. And part of his agenda included giving $5. 25 million to 25 media groups between 2003 and 2015.

Gill told *Rolling Stone* "we're going to punish the wicked" on the "religious right" as part of a shift to focus on nondiscrimination.

(Strange, that forcing others to believe as you do, is applauded by their agenda and yet intolerable if others do it. That seems like discrimination to me!)

According to *Rolling Stone,* Gill is "the nation's most powerful force for LGBTQ rights."

"So, here we are America, being a Christian is now "**wicked**." So, if Christians are **wicked**, according to Gill, how soon will it be that Christianity will be **outlawed** in America? If Gill is successful, as he was in Georgia with threatening economic sanctions, what happens in America? I mean we have the BDS (Boycott, Divest and Sanctions) movement being levied against Israel and now the same here in America against Christians. This is nothing more than economic blackmail, and what is interesting is these sick people don't even attempt to hide it."

Having moral standards because of one's faith is now deemed "**wicked**?" To believe that marriage is between one man and one woman but supportive of civil unions is cause for derision and attack?"

I believe Isaiah prophesied this when he declared:

Woe (judgment is coming) to those who call evil good, and good evil;

Who substitute darkness for light and light for darkness?

Who substitute bitter for sweet and sweet for bitter!

3. Rebellion Revered As Righteousness

If you watch the news especially sports news, entertainment news, or even religious news; you can see many examples where rebellion is revered. Whether it is a sports figure kneeling during the national anthem or actors promoting their anti-Bible biases in the political arena using their fan base to enlarge a political support base. Rebellion is seen as being intelligent, independent and involved. Rebellion is seen as a sign of leadership. Rebellion is seen as courageously opening the envelope of restrictive morals in order to liberate the youth.

But what does the Bible say about rebellion?

Rebellion is as sinful as witchcraft, and stubbornness as bad as worshiping idols. 1 Samuel 15:23 NLT

We have become a society where doing wrong is applauded. Because of the democratization of righteousness, wrong has become right and right has become wrong! When we vote on moral issues, we seldom vote based on truth but rather based on what makes things easier for us or what portrays our behavior as less reprehensible. What better way to pacify one's conscience than to vote evil as legal thus legitimizing corrupt character and unrestrained passion. If we can convince ourselves that if something is legal it is also moral and righteous, then the democratic process can easily redefine truth, character and even righteousness. ***In reality, our opinions do not matter, our vote is powerless, and our attempt to legitimize immorality futile.***

"Without the sun, there would be no sense of direction and without the Son, humanity would be lost!"

Chapter Twelve

Moral Mayhem

As a former teacher in the public school system, I was mandated to teach from a position of moral neutrality.

Education was supposed to be bias free, religion free and values neutral. We were not supposed to speak our opinion but merely teach the content of the curriculum. But in essence that was also a bias. From what perspective and whose opinion resulted in this particular curriculum?

What was their bias? What was their political ideology?

And what were they trying to communicate through that particular curriculum?

Is there such a thing as being totally unbiased?

How do we merely teach the curriculum without adding our values, personality, and experiences into the education process?

Since we are all moral beings, with emotions, thoughts and experiences, ***without a moral compass the result is confusion and chaos.*** We have entered the realm of moral mayhem in all of its destructive dimensions.

There are number of consequences to living in moral mayhem. Let me share a few:

- Nothing Is Absolute except Confusion
- Defiant Depravity Replaces Dignity
- Feelings Determine Beliefs Rather Than Beliefs Guiding Feelings

- Values and Behavior Are Reduced to the Lowest Common Denominator
- Freedom to Self-Destruct Is Saluted
- Pleasure Has Replaced Purpose
- *Searching for Meaning While Embracing the Randomness of Evolution*
- Nothingness Is Embraced Instead of Substance
- *The futile quest to reconcile one's search for significance while still believing they are primordial accidents*

Let's look at these in more detail.

Our educational system and our political system have embraced moral relativism and situational ethics. They declare there are no absolutes. And yet by making that declaration, they are making an ABSOLUTE pronouncement.

Without absolutes, impulse replaces integrity. There are no moorings on which to anchor a drifting ship. The ship represents your life; the ocean waves represent situational ethics and the mooring represents absolute truths. And when there is no mooring, **your life drifts away from shore into the ocean of meaninglessness**.

When we fail to see intrinsic value in every human being, defiant depravity will replace dignity. Bullying will increase, self-harm will increase, bizarre sexual activity will be lauded as freedom of expression, and mass shootings.

What is a tragedy if there is more moral absolutes? What is an act of evil, if there is no such thing as absolute right and wrong?

How do we measure atrocities if we are all evolutionary accidents randomly seeking meaning and purpose in a meaningless cosmos with no moral gravity to keep us grounded?

Has anyone ever experienced this emotional roller coaster?

How about having feelings of both love and hate towards the same person in the same day and maybe even within the same hour?

Our feelings? Would it be safe to say that basing our beliefs on something that erratic and volatile could be considered unwise?

Yet, we are living in a society that anchors their beliefs on their emotional state. Dangerous! "***If it feels good, do it!***" We've all heard that slogan haven't we?

Does feeling something automatically make it right?

What if one person feels like beating up the other person but that other person feels like living in harmony, whose feelings will win? Feelings will COLLIDE!

What if all married couples or sports players always made their behavioral decisions based on their feelings in the moment?

That is why I propose that truth, absolute truth, must dictate behavior, beliefs, and emotions.

Remember, even sailors many years ago needed a North Star to navigate their ships.

How much more do we need a North Star to guide society today?

Whenever we try to please everyone, our policies regarding moral standards will gravitate to the **lowest common denominator**.

You see, values and behavior are very much like the law of gravity

– **They are PULLED downward!**

This has been easily seen in our society over the last number of years. Behaviors not even thought of are now considered normal. Culture becomes more and more permissive. Our culture wants to call it being "more open-minded" which sound more positive than permissive. The term, "***permissive***" alludes to the fact that there is a moral code of right and wrong. They are just being lenient in the "wrongness" of it. We have become INCREASINGLY MORE strict in Drinking and Driving laws while at the same time becoming more lenient on illegal drugs. Apparel that was not acceptable on TV just a number of years ago, are now seen regularly worn at Junior High Schools.

Just imagine when my mother gave birth to me, that she would live to see the day when a man could walk into a woman's washroom merely by declaring that they gender-identify as a woman. I dare say that was not at all on her mind.

I grew up during a time when a handshake was as good as gold. If you made a deal with someone and you shook on it, it was a done deal! You could go to the bank on it. As a matter of fact, you could go home and have a peaceful night sleep not worrying at all about being ripped off.

I do not have to mention to you, that this is no longer true today. Today, we need contracts analyzed by lawyers in order to protect our business and our money. But even with that precaution, we're not safe because there are numerous scams out there that also get legal counsel on how they can take advantage of trusting individuals.

As are matter-of-fact, it happened to me. I was offered a contract and I tried to do the right thing by having a lawyer evaluate it. The lawyer evaluated the contract and analyzed the details. The lawyer deemed the contract valid and the company legit. On this advice, I entered into that contract and in less than a month I lost $1600. 00.

I can give another example of a contractor who was doing renovations for someone and after the renovations were complete, the person refused to pay - claiming that the renovator had done a terrible job. On that project alone the renovator lost $20,000.

The days of trust are gone because business relationships are swiftly moving towards the lowest common denominator!

There was a time when people were committed to relationship: now they are committed to money!

Even children tend to be more loyal to possessions and money than they are loyal to their parents!

This has not only affected business, it has also really impacted marriage. Who would have envisioned pre-nuptial agreements 30 years ago? Marriage used to be an act of total trust and commitment, now it has become a **calculated risk with benefits**.

Today, marriage is anchored firmly in the shifting sands of feelings!

Let's take a brief test to check the progress of this new "freedom". Let's evaluate the results of these societal moral changes

Please answer the following questions with the first thought that comes to your mind.	Circle
Is society HAPPIER, healthier and more optimistic now?	Y or N
Has the growing permissive leniency resulted in a more FULFILLED society?	Y or N
Has Peace, Harmony and Togetherness Improved?	Y or N

Has this moral leniency produced more respect towards one another?	Y or N
Has bullying decreased because of our relaxed moral codes?	Y or N
What about broken hearts, betrayal and depression? Have the incidences of these decreased because of the new leniency?	Y or N
Has this leniency lessened our guilt, regrets, and shame?	Y or N
Has it made society stronger and more resilient?	Y or N
Has self-esteem, self-respect and confidence increased because of the relaxed interpretation of right and wrong?	Y or N
Has loneliness decreased because of all the communication possibilities available to us?	Y or N

Let's talk briefly about Loneliness and Communication. We no longer have to wait a week or more to receive a letter from the person courting us. (People are too busy tapping this, tapping that and hooking up!)

We no longer have to talk to our boyfriend or girlfriend on a corded phone attached to the wall in the kitchen.

We can know more about a person with a few Snapchat, Facetime and Facebook activities than previous generations could discover in months or maybe years. This communication power should result in ***better communication, better relationship*** and ***better intimacy in marriage***.

John Maxwell, has written a book entitled, *Everyone Communicates, Few Connect*. Technology has the ability to increase your communication power but it cannot produce true soul to soul connection. You can have 1000 FB friends, YouTube subscribers, LinkedIn connections, and a huge contact list while still **suffocating from loneliness**.

Communication does not alleviate Loneliness - only true connection does.

Then there is the curse of texting. Other than the fact that it seems that it is illegal to walk across the street without texting or at least talking on their cell. (How did people cross the street before the advent of the cellphone?) I thought that POS stood for Point of Sale but to many youth it means **P**arent **O**ver **S**houlder. Then there is "Thot". Again, I was under the impression that THOT was an idea but our youth use that to refer to "**T**hat **h**oe **o**ver **t**here".

When you hear or see "***Netflix and chill***" what comes to your mind? Well, it actually means "***Let's get together and hook up***" Hook up means casual sex or sex without dating or friends with benefits who are not dating or committed to each other. And I thought Netflix and chill meant let's watch a movie together and relax! My, was I wrong!

Here are just a few more hidden messages –

- LH6 (Let's have sex);
- IWSN (I want sex now);

- MPFB (My personal **** buddy);
- KYS (kill yourself);
- GNOC (get naked on camera);
- 8 (oral sex); 99 (parents are gone);
- CU46 (see you for sex);
- PAW (parents are watching);
- KPS (Keep parents clueless);
- and LMIRL (Let's meet in real life)

Our youth's secret communications are dangerous and fanning the flame of risky destructive behavior!

In our neighborhood, just over a year ago, something tragic happened. Actually, many tragic things have happened but I just want to focus on this one.

There was a bright guy and a bright gal who were dating. They were 16 but they had been dating since they were 13. The guy decided to break off the relationship because it was getting too serious. That Friday, the girl committed suicide because her purpose in life was gone. (The curse of premature emotional attachment). On Saturday, the guy heard the terrible news. He was FLOODED with GUILT and killed himself on Sunday.

What a weekend! What a waste!
What a tragedy! What a consequence of moral leniency.

They were too close, too intimate, too attached, and too YOUNG! Their emotional maturity was not developed enough to handle all the emotions, feelings and confusion that were bombarding their hearts and minds.

When this happens, there are several possible responses.

• Some commit suicide like this couple.

• Others react by being promiscuous and participating in very risky behavior.

• Yet others just become hard and stop caring about other people's feelings except to use them, take advantage of them and manipulate them for their own selfish purposes.

• Still others cope by abusing drugs and alcohol.

Then there is the final group

They hurt, they feel immense pain and they are confused. Their heart is broken. They respond by trying to understand what is happening, embracing the pain as a teaching moment. They use the pain to learn how to guard their heart and choose a path of healing.

They choose to learn from pain, so that in the future they will be able to love fully, care deeply and trust completely in the right relationship.

Their RESPONSE not REACTION looks something like this:

- Caution without Bitterness.
- Hope without Impulsivity.

- Patience without being Inactive in life.
- Loving others without being Vulnerable.
- Elevate their Standards and Self-esteem without being disconnected.

Truth over Emotion. Purpose over Passion. Future over Failure. Long-term over Temporary. And Growth over Giving Up!

Unfortunately, this group is in the minority, possibly to the point of being on the ENDANGERED species list!

The new moral leniency actually encourages REACTION rather than RESPONSE and results in REGRETS instead of RESPECT!

They promote "***If it feels good, do it!***" and then when things go wrong – PANIC!!

It could be an unplanned pregnancy, or that dreaded STI, or vehicular homicide while driving impaired.

One of the dangerous parts of this new moral leniency is they ***ANNOUNCE*** *very loudly* – ***FREEDOM of CHOICE*** *but then whisper (so no one can hear) the immense* ***COST of CONSEQUENCES!***

NEWS ALERT

We cannot choose the consequences!

Many times our reckless choices and experimentation are our feeble attempt at feeling significant.

It actually is a setup for even greater ***insignificance***!

When you ***Search for Significance*** without possessing a Healthy Self-Esteem, you'll seek Significance in all the **WRONG** places, therefore sabotaging True Significance.

It could be in your career, your relationships, your body image, your wealth, your prestige, your sexual exploits, your athletic accomplishments, or your number of FB friends.

The problem with these attempts to embrace significance is that they are outside of your control, therefore making you a victim to circumstances.

When you lack control - your significance and self-esteem are in jeopardy.

You could lose your career due to downsizing; your significant other could leave you; an accident could destroy your looks; a recession could evaporate your wealth; Time could run out on your 15 minutes of fame; and injury could eliminate your athletic future in a split second! That is why,

---

Significance needs to come from the inside!

Reactionary decision making through your feelings, your circumstances or your selfishness very seldom produces excellence and more often produces chaos and a trail of broken dreams.

ARK Angel Manifesto

Society's moral leniency elevates (feelings, group think, hormones, and adrenalin) above TRUTH and the priceless value of themselves and others! There is a biblical principle that the Moral Leniency movement needs to understand. It is found in Mark 12:31.

"Love your neighbor as yourself"

If you run your life on the fuel of feelings and situations you encounter, there will be a long list of regrets, disappointments, shame and guilt. This could lead you to self-hatred and it often does (but you probably have learned ways to disguise it well).

Now if you are to love those around you with the SAME level of love you have for yourself, you could very well be an instrument of increased pain and suffering in the world. If your self-love is not based on the TRUTH and the immense VALUE every human being possesses - respect, appreciation, understanding, and community will disappear.

ABUSE will become epidemic!

How does a person truly love themselves when they believe that they are an accident? This is the dilemma that the Moral Leniency Movement must wrestle with. How does one promote an improved quality of life by demoting humanity from being created in the Image of God to a primordial accident?

Moral Mayhem is a cancer and it is malignant!

The books that the world calls immoral are books that show the world its own shame.

Oscar Wilde,

Unless we discover actual truth, morality is up for grabs.

Pamela Christian

Chapter Thirteen

Political Pathology & Educational Entropy

Politicians are leaders! They are the face of a country or constituency for the world to see. You tend to JUDGE people by the politician that they voted into power. Politicians like the entertainment industry tend to set the direction for society. They are role models for this generation and next!

Their decisions, their values, and their agendas are the yarn that weaves the fabric of the future!

Political Pathology

Pathology – suffering from a disease which has become a medical disorder. Politics is in a state of ill-health. It should actually be classified as a mental disorder. There are many pathogens invading the political body. It has become pathological.

In our technological world of indecent exposure, the media bombards us with images, sound bites and salacious details of hidden agendas revealed! Isn't it interesting just how many TV programs are dedicated to the political theme? Politics and the Entertainment Media have entered into a very strange open marriage. In the past, there were numerous crime dramas and comedy programs but very few direct politically themed programs. Chuck Tryon on August 25, 2016 wrote the following in Mental Floss:

"Historically, during the network era, broadcasters tended to shy away from controversial political material, but in recent decades – thanks in part to cable and streaming video – we've seen TV shows featuring captivating political content flourish."

What has emerged over that number of years?

- West Wing
- House of Cards
- Madam Secretary
- Scandal
- Homeland
- The Americans
- Suits
- Designated Survivor
- Quantico

So what are the characteristics of our present political scene? It seems that they are role modeling the following:

- **Insanity** not Wisdom
- **Corruption** not Conscience
- **Bullying** not Brotherhood
- **Manipulation** not Morale
- **Deception** not Transparency

- **Distortion** not Clarity
- **Broken Promises** not Integrity
- **Using people** not Leading them
- **Entitlement** not Empathy
- **Popularity Contests** not Personal Character
- **Power** not Principles
- **Self-aggrandizement** not Servant Leadership

IF this is the nature of their role modeling, what does the future hold?

I believe that this is where the Church comes in. In the next Section, I will discuss the challenge and responsibility of the Church during these turbulent times.

The Church must rise up and prepare to be an ARK for the drowning.

Just as a thought, what would happen IF the Church exemplified the RIGHT side of the above list?

A) Not only has Politics married the Entertainment Industry, they have also married Education. Education used to be a platform for thought and character but since the marriage with Politics, it has been sadly more focused on **propaganda** and **globalism**. Education used to be a system to prepare for independence and maturity. Now it is used more for the subtle creation of followers and the celebration of unrestrained experience. At the college level immaturity, recklessness and moral experimentation are celebrated and actually encouraged.

I remember even many years ago when I was at university, 30 years ago. (WOW that makes me feel old!).

I had borrowed a Christian tape (before the time of CD's) from Michelle, a student at the same university. She lived in the Women's dorm. I promised to return it so I went to the dorm and asked the woman at the desk if they could contact Michelle so I could return the tape.

The woman told me Michelle's dorm room number and said I could bring it to her. Then she said,

"You are welcome to stay the night with Michelle, we just need you to sign in so we know the number of occupants to comply with the fire code regulation".

All I wanted to do was return a Christian tape to Michelle. The thought of staying the night NEVER crossed my mind and yet the education system was promoting immaturity and immorality.

It's no wonder that a recent statistic reveals that **7 out of 10** first-year college students raised in a Christian home who professed faith in Jesus Christ, abandoned their faith before they graduated from college/university!

As with the political pathology that I have just described, the educational system is also suffering from what they have sown. I could go into detail by analyzing the evolution of the educational system. That will be another book.

Educational Entropy

Entropy is a process of degeneration marked variously by increasing degrees of uncertainty, disorder, fragmentation, chaos, etc., such a process regarded as the inevitable, terminal stage in the life of a social system or structure.

So what is the educational system manufacturing in our times?

Here is a list:

Blind Followers Not Great Thinkers.

Great thinkers challenge the status quo and the agenda of those trying to create the world in their own image. Blind followers are rewarded, complemented, affirmed so they can become eager participants in a destructive agenda that they are not aware of. Blind followers are applauded as heroes as they march in unison to their own demise.

Dependence Not Leadership.

If the education system can create a sense of dependence that looks like independence, they can create a massive army of "worker bees" willing to sacrifice themselves for a cause they know nothing about. When you really look at it, our education system is threatened by true leadership.

Cloning Not Individuality.
Look-alike, think alike, behave alike in order to be liked! This is a recipe for acceptance because we have become a culture that is threatened by individuality and expends much energy to eradicate it. We are a culture that seemingly applauds diversity and at same time seeks to squash freedom of speech, freedom of assembly, freedom of religion and freedom of belief. We have a difficulty of valuing individuals or groups that believe differently than us. We see that as a battleground.

Social Conformity Not Mutual Respect.
Therefore, social conformity and not mutual respect of individuals is the hidden agenda that when achieved will be able to control the world. Education is becoming a critical component in creating the building blocks for a **ONE WORLD** government.

Social Engineering Not True Self-Awareness
Social engineering becomes the educational system's mandate and mission statement.

- Its purpose is to create groupthink.
- Its purpose is to make conformity attractive.
- Its purpose is to make "thinking outside the box" something to fear.
- Its purpose is to encourage students to focus on the external, and dismiss the inner-self and the eternal.
- Its purpose is to make self-esteem based on approval and acceptance by the merchandisers of the New World order.

- When self-esteem is based on true self-awareness, individuals are not easily manipulated and controlled.

Therefore, these confident, creative, character centered individuals become a threat!

Agenda Based Learning Not TRUTH-based Foundation.

Casual attitude regarding spiritual truth not a mastery attitude.

- Casual **beliefs** and casual **values** as being fluid, not anchored to absolutes. Social values are drifting in whatever direction the waves of feelings and impulses are going.
- Casual **sex** where oneness and true intimacy are trashed for the sake of depraved imaginations, and exciting experiences.
- Casual **responsibility** that doesn't take commitment and duty seriously. Responsibility is an option that must bow to the SELF-IMPOSED authority of instant gratification.
- Casual **relationships** that are based on convenience and self-interest.
- Casual **ethics** that basis decisions not on what is right but rather what is appealing to the person at that particular moment.

- Therefore, lying, cheating, and deception become moral virtues if they help a person advance along the path of their personal agenda. **In casual ethics, the individual becomes the Standard of Truth.**

Therefore, cheating in order to get a promotion; sleeping with a superior in order to advance your career; lying on an insurance claim in order to get more benefits, **all become honorable within the casual ethics paradigm.**

EVERYTHING IS CASUAL EXCEPT THE CONSEQUENCES

Experience Not Excellence.

We have become a culture that celebrates experiences and we have removed the moral parameters of experiences. In many ways, experiences have become our God. We worship experiences, we chase after experiences and we even evaluate the quality of our lives based on the number and variety of experiences we have had. In past cultures, excellence was celebrated and measured by – excellence in learning, excellence in character, excellence in integrity, excellence in loyalty, excellence in relationships, excellence in leadership and excellence in wisdom.

Excuse Based Mediocrity Not Acceptance of Responsibility.

We're living in the times of blaming. Instead of accepting responsibility for their choices, they would rather blame it on society, their parents, and their ethnicity or their socio-economic condition. Whenever mediocrity is challenged, they make excuses believing that entitles them to avoid all the consequences. ***So now mediocrity is becoming the new standard.*** It is actually even embraced as wisdom by many people. You know them as the people at work who do just enough not to get fired and who do no more than the minimum of expectations. And then they continually complain that they are not getting the promotions that they want.

This results in a **Culture Based** Not Character Based world view and belief system.

When looking at our culture's political, entertainment, media, educational, ethics and business persona, this section could continue endlessly providing examples of infractions with dangerous implications.

I believe that you could fill the pages yourself with examples. Therefore, this will suffice as evidence that times have seriously changed.

From climate change, to moral change, to family structure change, to technology change, to political change, to educational change, to theological change – we can see that we are now living in turbulent times!

Also the speed of change is happening more rapidly all the time. Our minds, emotions and energy are on the brink of overload and becoming MAXED out!

Adapting, adjusting, and accommodating to this rapid change is resulting in unbearable stress, fear, anxiety and numbness. It's becoming more and more difficult to cope and the waves of inner and outer pressure are crashing against our souls! The undercurrents are dragging many people under. The tsunami of cultural implosion is creating massive ripple effects around the world.

People unable to cope and adapt to the changing world are responding with extremism!

The ***Spirit of Christ*** is calling forth ARK Angels to be messengers of Hope, Peace, and Protection in these ***Turbulent Times***!

The next section will attempt to EQUIP believers who desire to be ARK Angels in a hurting and turbulent world! As they discover and discipline their specific Spirit-filled Divine Assignment of ARK building, their IMPACT on this generation will be miraculous!

Part THREE
The ARK Angel Manifesto

Where the Kingdom of God meets the Turbulence of our Times

If we only had eyes to see and ears to hear and wits to understand - we would know that the Kingdom of God (in the sense of holiness, goodness, beauty) is as close as breathing and is crying out to born both within ourselves and within the world and we would know that the Kingdom of God is what we all hunger for above all other things even when we don't know its name or realize that it's what we're starving to death for.

Frederick Buechner

Chapter Fourteen

The Kingdom of God–ARK Construction

A child is busy building something with *Lego.* When they are finished, they call for you to look at their masterpiece. You look at it, and say "what is it?" The child responds by saying, "***can't you see, it's our house***!"

Many people see the church this way. They look at and ask, "What is it?" In many ways the church is a mess. That is why there is a clarion call for a ***Noah Revolution!***

I believe that there is a key connection and relationship between Noah and the mandate of the Church. As we mentioned at the beginning of the book, Noah means **REST**.

From the biblical account, no matter what was going on around Noah, he seemed to find that place where he could hear God and know the timing of the Lord. He lived in a state of emotional and spiritual rest even when the moral and social climate around him was tumultuous.

The title of this book, is ***The ARK Angel Manifesto*** and demonstrates the vital need for "ark" builders in this generation. I placed the words Ark and Angel together for a very specific reason – the word Angel means messenger and the ark symbolizes ***protection, provision, deliverance, and victory***.

Therefore, ARK Angel means Messengers of Hope, Peace, Protection, Provision, Deliverance and Victory in a Culture of Chaos & Confusion!!
We as individual Christians and as a Church, are to be clear messengers and guides for lost, confused and drowning individuals and cultures!

Our message must be a message of hope, peace, and deliverance in a turbulent world. But a message is not enough (if Noah had just shared messages and messages and more messages but did not actively gather wood and follow the construction plans of God to actually build the ark, no one would've been saved).

We must also provide a solution by being experienced guides in order to lead (actively and intentionally) lead people to safety, security and salvation!

So the question is, why ARK Angels?

"The greatest threat to civil society is mankind. Every day the flood of images on our television screens tells the sad story. Blood, death, diplomacy, conflict, hatred, fear, poverty, starvation, rape, genocide, refugees and human migration, natural disasters, daily bombings, economic uncertainty, immigration, corporate corruption, moral decay, sexual revolution, and clash of counter culture's – all of these testify to the undeniable fact that we are our own worst enemy.

"Kingdom Principles, 11

ARK Angel Manifesto

"All of our universities, cyber-space technology, black-berries, think tanks, G-8 meetings, fiscal and immigration policies, medical advancements, social experiments, religious conferences, peace marches, and declarations of cease-fire and peace on earth all seem to collapse at the mercy of our own self-imposed destructive spirit. We build buildings and then bomb them; we make weapons and then use them on ourselves; we invent medicines that heal and then withhold them from the sick; we improve the World Wide Web to enhance global communication and then use it to destroy the moral fiber of our children. We are our own greatest enemy."

Myles Monroe, Kingdom Principles, 11

We today are living in a climate of moral and social upheaval! That is a huge reason we need ARK Angels!

Here is just one example from a not very large community. We are not talking Las Vegas, Los Angeles, Bangkok, New Orleans, Rio de Janeiro, New York, Manila, Madrid, Caracas, or Mexico City. We are talking about a medium size conservative Midwest city.

A personal friend of mine has a fellow employee who demonstrates this climate very graphically. His after work occupation, as if that is what you would call it, is to cater to the sexual desires of his over 200 female clients. 80% of his clients are married. They are lawyers, judges, senior government officials, teachers, nurses and many other professional careers are represented. As he is confiding with my friend, he admits that he is bored. You see, he has unlimited access to sex. And yet he is empty, unfulfilled, lonely and living with no real sense of purpose. He tells my friend that he is envious of him because he is a one woman man. Yet he admits he could never be faithful to the woman he loved.

He is searching but never finding – his pleasures are becoming his paralysis, and prison in regards to his emotional, spiritual and possibly even physical well-being. Now you think of this man was a fairly young man, but you would be wrong. This man is approaching retirement.

I believe that this single excerpt of a middle-aged man gives you a glimpse of the times of Noah. I also believe that the mandate and mission of the Church is to help these restless souls find rest and to help these purposeless people find their divine purpose.

I believe that in the end times, the Church will be the contact point between God and a floundering and faithless people! The Church will be where the lost, confused and hurting can receive **REST** from

- Their labors,
- From their sin,

- From their brokenness,
- From their shame
- From their sickness,
- From their diseases,
- From poverty,
- From the things of this world and
- From the turmoil in their spirit.

If the Church's character and focus would reflect the Ark that it is called to be - multitudes of restless and lost people will enter the Ark of PROTECTION and PURPOSE!

When Noah heard the Word of the Lord, he responded immediately and totally. He put all of his resources and energy into building, which became both a warning to his carnal and confused generation plus divine deliverance for him and his family.

Radicals on the other hand, would not allow free will! Either they would force people into the ark or they would systematically punish individuals who did not see things the way the radicals did.

Noah in this sense is a type of God because he respects the WILL of individuals even though he knows their choice will be very devastating.

ARK Angel Manifesto

The metaphor of Ark builders (ARK Angels) is really the Church's commitment to expand and advance the Kingdom of God. So whenever I will mention *"we need to build an ark"* what I'm saying is, we need to get serious about the Kingdom of God not merely our personal ticket to heaven.

You cannot be a tourist in the Kingdom of God! There are no cruise ships or cruises! Just an Ark of Deliverance in the midst of a storm!

There are a few things that we need to know about ARK builders.

First of all, they are NOT RELIGIOUS.

Secondly, they are COUNTER CULTURAL.

Thirdly, they are NOT THEORETICAL. Rather, they are activists in the most compassionate sense. They are BUILDERS not merely believers.

Fourthly, they will be CONSPICUOUS and talked about.

Fifthly, they are CONSISTENT and do not waver because of peer pressure.

And finally, they are CONFIDENT! They have clearly heard from God and that obedience is their ONLY option! Their actions and choices are NOT based on their personal opinions but rather on Powerful Oracles from God!

ARK Angels as stated before are not religious and do not promote religious duty, traditions, customs and rituals.

So what is the difference between ARK Angels (Kingdom Builders) and the religious leader? How can we distinguish between the Kingdom of Heaven and religion?

• Religion **preoccupies** humans until they find the Kingdom. It keeps them busy trying to please God.

• Religion is what people **do** until they find the Kingdom.

• Religion prepares humanity to leave Earth; the Kingdom empowers people to dominate earth.

• Religion focuses on Heaven; the Kingdom focuses on the King of Kings' presence on Earth.

• Religion is reaching up to God; the Kingdom is God coming down to mankind.

• Religion wants to escape Earth; the Kingdom impacts, influences and changes Earth.

• Religion seeks to take earth to Heaven; the Kingdom seeks to bring Heaven to Earth. Kingdom Principles, 18-19

So what actually is the kingdom?
Someone has said that the Kingdom of God is the realm where the reign and rule of God is in full operation.

A kingdom requires a king, a ruler whose reign is absolute.

This means the King is not vulnerable to popular opinion or the values of the masses. He is a leader with full power and authority.

Therefore, the King of Kings, ***desires his kingdom to come on Earth as it already is in heaven***. He also ***desires to establish his kingdom in every believer's heart***!

The late Myles Munroe, defined *a Kingdom* this way:

A Kingdom is the governing influence of a king over his territory impacting it with his personal will, purpose, and intent, producing a culture, values, morals, and lifestyle that reflects the Kings desires and nature for his citizens.

So why is the Kingdom of God so important? Well, in Matthew 6:33, it says," but seek first His and Kingdom His Righteousness, and all these things will be given to you as well. "This advice comes right after the previous two versus which say," so do not worry, saying, 'what shall we eat?' or' what shall we drink?' or' what shall we wear?' For the pagans **RUN** after all these things, and your heavenly Father knows that you need them. "

When we look at the numerous billboards while driving, or the commercials while watching TV or the pop-ups while surfing the net, we see our generation running after all these things - as if the mere act of accumulation gives life purpose. It also almost appears that the chasing after these things is much like the evacuation chaos of a public arena right after a bomb threat! Their life depends on it!

And as I was pondering this verse, I started wondering what percentage of commercials are advertising **food**, **drinks**, and **clothing**. Maybe I should do a study on these statistics of advertising, but from my observation, I would be willing to hazard a guess that those three areas would dominate over 75% of all TV advertising.

But, the advice that we are given is to seek first His

Kingdom and His Righteousness. This means **it is God's number one priority for humanity**. In this verse, Jesus identifies the Kingdom as being more important than food, water, clothing, shelter, and every other basic human need.

"This declaration by Jesus also suggests that there must be something about the Kingdom that all of mankind has missed and misunderstood. If everything we perceive, pursue and strive for in order to live and survive are found in the Kingdom, then we have been misguided and perhaps have imposed on ourselves unnecessary hardship, stress, and frustration."

Myles Munroe, "Kingdom Principles" p. 29

This verse also advises us to seek His Righteousness. So what is His Righteousness? And since it comes right after the concept of kingdom. We have to understand righteousness from a kingdom perspective.

In reality, righteousness is not a religious concept but rather a **governmental** concept. "In essence, righteousness describes the maintenance of the ***rightly aligned relationship with a governing authority*** in order to qualify for the right to receive governmental privileges. This is why Jesus emphasizes the Kingdom and the need to be righteous, so that you can receive

'All things added unto you'. This promise **includes:**

- ✓ ***ALL your physical needs,***
- ✓ ***ALL your social needs,***
- ✓ ***All your emotional needs,***
- ✓ ***All your psychological needs,***
- ✓ ***ALL your financial needs, and***
- ✓ ***ALL your security needs,***
- ✓ ***As well as your need for self-significance and a sense of self-worth and purpose. "Kingdom Principles, 31-32***

Noah was described as a righteous man, meaning he was rightly aligned with the governing authority of the King of Kings! That means that all these things were added unto him.

Chapter Fifteen

Patience of an ARK Angel

When Noah heard the Word of the Lord, he took immediate action! As I mentioned a few pages back, this project took time.

It reminds me when I was a boy living on the farm. One adventurous day, a couple of us red-necked farm boys decided to build a raft and so we could float and paddle it on our large pond. We gathered some logs and some twine and some rope and hammers and even nails. Then we got to work. We were industrious. Well, at first we were industrious and then we became impatient like young boys often are.

You see we weren't focused on building the ark. We wanted to have fun floating and paddling the raft on the pond. So we took shortcuts, so we could start enjoying the raft on the pond. These shortcuts meant inferior construction but we did have idealism and impatience. When impatience won over logic, we pushed that raft into the water and we gleefully with anticipation climbed onto the raft preparing ourselves for fun, excitement, and experience. There was some excitement and there was a lot of experience but there was very little fun!

The water in the pond was still and calm with no ripples to be found. Yet, in but a few moments our compromised workmanship was exposed. The logs and boards began to separate, and we began to sink. In a split second, we went from being young boys on top of the water to young boys under the water! We were hanging onto the logs that were floating us away in different directions. We struggled to the shore and chalked that event to experience.

We had not prepared properly. The conditions were ideal and yet we sank.

Noah on the other hand, did prepare properly and even under treacherous conditions beyond our wildest imagination remained afloat!

Chapter Sixteen

Commitment of an ARK Angel

After hearing the Word of the LORD, the first thing Noah had to do was count the cost. Willingness to count the cost was a key characteristic of Noah!

This is exactly where the ARK Angels must begin! Just as Noah, knowing full well he would have to depend daily on God to get the job done, he still chose to obey. He also knew this was not a weekend project or a small item on one's to-do list. His project was not a canoe building kit that would take just weeks to complete and then off to the lake to enjoy nature.

NO! This was a lifelong commitment!

This reminds me of a cute story about a conversation between a pig and chicken. The taken the chicken had escaped the farmyard and as they approached the town they saw a restaurant with a big sign on it. And these are very intelligent animals because they could read.

And they read the sign on the restaurant window.

The sign said

BREAKFAST SPECIAL

Bacon (4 slices) served with 2 ranch fresh eggs. Your choice of either Home Style Fries, hash browns, or grits. You also can choose between toast and freshly baked biscuits. For ONLY $1 extra enjoy one of our Famous Pancakes or Waffles!

The Pig and the Chicken looked in the window. What they saw SHOCKED them! On every table, the centerpiece looked uncomfortably familiar! (a pig and chicken as salt n pepper shakers)

The pig looked at the chicken and said,

"This is not fair! To make these people happy, you merely have to give a contribution but for me, it's a TOTAL COMMITMENT!"

There are a lot of "chickens" in the Church! They flock together to a gathering and if they have something to give, they will contribute.

Now the ARK Angels are more like the pig in this analogy. For them, there is no turning back! For them, it requires death, not contribution!

ARK Angels must really count the cost.

Let's explore this by examining Luke 14:27-33

"If you don't carry your own cross with the confident commitment of marching to your own execution when you follow Me, you can't be part of My movement. Just imagine that you want to build a tower. Wouldn't

you first sit down and estimate the cost to be sure you have enough to finish what you start? If you lay the foundation but then can't afford to finish the tower, everyone will mock you: "Look at that guy who started something that he couldn't finish!"

Or imagine a king gearing up to go to war.

Wouldn't he begin by sitting down with his advisors to determine whether his 10,000 troops could defeat the opponent's 20,000 troops? If not, he'll send a peace delegation quickly and negotiate a peace treaty. In the same way, if you want to be My disciple, it will cost you everything. Don't underestimate that cost!" The Voice (emphasis mine)

When we look more closely at this biblical account, we notice what commitment really is.

"Whoever does not carry his own cross and come after Me cannot be My disciple."

What is carrying your own cross mean anyway?

Great question!

Many people believe that this means the willingness to die.

I believe that it is actually the OPPOSITE!

I believe that carrying your own cross is a willingness to LIVE!

Let me explain. In the crucifixion, what does the cross represent for Jesus?

- *Payment for the sins of the world*
- *Canceling the curse of Adam*

- *Initiating a new blood covenant for ALL who believe*
- *Exchanging His life in order to give us TRUE LIFE*

In summary, the cross represented Christ Jesus' Divine Assignment!

Therefore, **our cross represents our Divine Assignment!**

Another way of saying it is – **your cross is God's purpose for your life!**

"For which one of you, when he wants to build a tower, does not first sit down and calculate the cost to see if he has enough to complete it? Otherwise, when he has laid a foundation and is not able to finish, all who observe it begin to ridicule him, saying, 'This man began to build and was not able to finish."

Noah counted the cost! When he began to build, he was committed to finishing what he started. He completed his Divine Assignment!

What was Esther's Divine Assignment? Advocating for the Jews. She counted the cost and protected the Jews from slaughter.

How about the 12 spies that were assigned to scout out the Promised Land? 10 made ONLY a contribution but 2 made the commitment to count the cost. Joshua and Caleb completed their Divine Assignment while the others died in the Wilderness.

You can see that taking up your cross is NOT about dying but LIVING!!

Who else counted the cost of their Divine Assignment? Ruth, Abraham, Joseph, Samuel, Apostle Paul, and many, many more throughout the pages of Scripture.

Now it is your turn, as ARK Angels, to count the cost, embrace your Divine Assignments and be instruments of true Deliverance!

So what does it mean to count the cost?

For the builder, of a tower in the biblical account; it meant finances, manpower, products, and supplies. But for the ARK Angel, it actually means something totally different. God has ALREADY provided all the resources for you to achieve your Divine Assignment and Purpose!

2 Peter 1:3 (AMP)

"For His divine power has bestowed on us [absolutely] everything necessary for [a dynamic spiritual] life and godliness, through true and personal knowledge of Him who called us by His own glory and excellence." Therefore, counting the cost of being an ARK Angel is easy right?

WRONG!

Even though God has given us EVERYTHING required for us to achieve our Divine Assignment and God's Purpose for our lives, there is ONE ingredient essential for activating all these resources and this ingredient is very, very, very costly!

Since God will supply ALL the resources and all the power required for us to SUCCEED in our Divine Assignment, we have no excuse for not achieving our Divine

Assignment. Yet many of us miss our Divine Assignment completely.

As a matter of fact, I missed mine for many years because of

- *Distractions,*
- *Unbelief,*
- *Low Self-esteem,*
- *False Guilt,*
- *Shame and*
- *Faulty Theology!*

The special ingredient that only you can add is your WILL!

God will add the rest!

God gives us His Word, His Power, His Authority, His Grace, His Faith, His Strength, His Favor and His Ability for us to do all that He's called us to do!

All He wants from you as ARK Angels, disciples, and believers is your WILLINGNESS!

When God gives you a revelation of your Divine Assignment and Purpose, you must count the cost to determine if you are WILLING to stay committed until your Divine Assignment is accomplished.

Just as Noah had to count the cost of building the ark for 100 years, if you are going to be an effective ARK Angel, you must also make a long-term commitment that goes far beyond feelings, circumstances, approval of others and your personal interests.

If you decide that you cannot make that level of commitment but are only really interested in periodic contribution to the cause of the Kingdom of God, you WILL compromise with the enemy! The enemy comes in different shapes and sizes. The enemy could be Satan's sinister agenda, material things, approval of people, the easy life, entertainment, entitlement and desire for no conflict.

Remember in Luke 14 where the king is facing a war.

Let me refresh your memory.

"Imagine a king gearing up to go to war.

Wouldn't he begin by sitting down with his advisors to determine whether his 10,000 troops could defeat the opponent's 20,000 troops? If not, he'll send a peace delegation quickly and negotiate a peace treaty."

This king really didn't want to fight for his kingdom, so if the victory wasn't guaranteed, he was willing to quickly concede his Divine Assignment to be the king, leader, and protector of his kingdom. He will compromise with the enemy. He will negotiate away his purpose, values, identity, and destiny that his kingdom represents. Remember, in those days, the kingdom represented the values, character, morals, beliefs, and agenda of the king. If the king is willing to negotiate that away, he is, in reality, relinquishing his identity.

In the same way, if you are not willing to protect the kingdom and count the cost of the fight, you will lose your identity as a Christ follower before the watching eyes of the world!

Future ARK Angels, get your heart monitor and calculator out! It's time to count the cost of your Divine Assignment.

Focus

One price you will have to pay is the price of FOCUS!

Nehemiah had a Divine Assignment.

Nevertheless, my journey continued until I reached Jerusalem. After three days in the city, under the cover of darkness, I was accompanied by a small group of men. The True God had placed a secret plan on my heart, and there I had left it hidden until the time was right. No one knew what it was I imagined for Jerusalem. Neh. 6:11-12 Voice

Let's back up a little in the story of Nehemiah. He heard the terrible news about his homeland. It was in shambles. Jerusalem was an unprotected, rubble-filled disaster. It was where his ancestors were buried. He loved his homeland and this news broke his heart.

Often our Divine Assignment is found in our deepest pain, greatest passion or most devastating defeat/failure!

Nehemiah's Divine Assignment was the city of Jerusalem. And where a Divine Assignment is discovered, an enemy or enemies WILL surface! Here is the Divine Assignment unfolding:

When the Assyrians conquered Israel's Northern Kingdom in 722 B. C., the Samaritans were exiled to other Assyrian provinces, and other Assyrian prisoners were settled in Samaria. Based on the etymology of their names, Sanballat's family is probably one of those relocated families who adopted the worship of the Eternal once they moved to Samaria.

Now, almost 300 years later, Sanballat is the first of his family appointed governor of Samaria under the Persians. Following 15 years of political unrest, he has managed to form a loose federation of Persian provinces in the area that includes Jerusalem. Tobiah is a Persian official who has taken care of Jerusalem until a new governor arrived. Now that Nehemiah has arrived, Sanballat's power over Jerusalem is uncertain. Nehemiah has not agreed to be part of his federation, so Jerusalem could become a threat to it.

Even though Nehemiah received the favor (of God and the King he served) plus received provision and protection, enemies would enter the drama seeking to alter the ending of the story.

This is also true for us as well. Once we discover our

Divine Assignment, we KNOW that God our King will provide us everything we need to complete our assignment. He also promises protection along the journey of fulfilling our assignment!

Nevertheless, the enemy will place stumbling blocks before you seeking to trip you up, fill you with fear and guide you to start rationalizing quitting the assignment.

What were the stumbling blocks that were thrown along the path of Nehemiah's purpose?

1) Social Distraction

"Sanballat and Geshem sent messengers to me.

Sanballat and Geshem's Message:

Come and meet with us in the plain of Ono, at the border village of Cheriphim. They were planning to hurt me." Neh. 6:2 Voice

This was a social invitation. They are saying in essence.

Nehemiah, you've been work so hard, it's time for a break. Let's hang out and get to know each other better. The last part of the verse says that they were planning to hurt Nehemiah. But Nehemiah didn't know this in the natural. They did not advertise their devious plans.

Nehemiah knew the scheme because he was in tune with the Spirit of God.

This reminds me of an event that happened when I was in grade eight. Alison, a neighbor girl, who was in grade nine was told about a party that was happening that weekend. She was the studious type and did not attend these parties. She also was very pretty but equally shy.

There was a desire to be accepted by the popular crowd so after an inner battle throughout the week, Alison finally on Friday afternoon, decided to go. She went to the party and at the party, her life changed.

The guys kept feeding her alcohol while encouraging her, complimenting her and validating her as part of the group. She became very drunk because she hadn't drunk alcohol before.

While she was drunk another first happened. Yes, she was raped. (They say it was consensual) but she was totally drunk so she could not give her consent. In reality, it was just sensual pleasure at her expense!

Another first that night was that Alison became pregnant!

Alison, the pretty, studious, shy teenager decided to quit school before the semester was over.

Social Distractions Are Powerful. We all long for acceptance and a sense of belonging. Maybe your social distraction is not as devastating as Alison's were but it still could sabotage your Divine Assignment. Social distractions are everywhere and are the most subtle stumbling block strategy.

In Nehemiah's case, the attempt at social distraction happened five times. ***Persistent peer-pressure is a strategy to wear you down and weaken your values and resolve***.

2) Gossip Distraction

Sanballat's Letter: A report has gone out to the surrounding nations that you are rebuilding the wall because you and your fellow Jews are planning to revolt against Persia. Geshem confirms this report and suggests you are looking to be crowned as king. Rumor has it that you have even appointed prophets to announce in Jerusalem, "Judah has a king!" referencing you. Be assured, this very report will make it back to King Artaxerxes. Meet with us at once. Neh. 6:6-7 Voice

They have upped the ante! Gossip is a powerful way to control people. Now, these people are creating a false problem and then offering themselves as the solution.

Devious and Tricky!

They are using documentation, information and even your personal values to pressure compliance.

Just think if they were in the cellphone era? Photo shopped pictures of Nehemiah with a crown on his head placed on Instagram, Facebook, etc. plus personally Messaging the King these convicting pictures portraying Nehemiah as a traitor.

Just imagine what takes place these days to distract a person from their Divine Assignment.

As you are reading this, do events in your life pop up in your mind? Do you now see them as sabotaging strategies seeking to derail you?

Many years ago, I went to Nebraska to visit my cousin

Merle. Even though he had to work, I hung out at his place until he got off work. We were planning something for the evening.

While waiting, I turned on the TV. There was a NEWS FLASH! It was the Miami Riots. I watched.

The reporter was telling us that the police were violently attacking the immigrants, beating them, and declaring that this abuse of new people to the USA must stop! The camera footage confirmed the report.

I flicked the channels and happened upon another NEWSFLASH about the Miami Riots. This reporter was telling us that the immigrants were attacking the police and the police were trying to defend themselves against the mob violence that they were caught in. The reporter continued to say that the immigrants were tipping over police cars and setting them on fire. The cameraperson for this reporter also confirmed the report with the equally convincing footage.

As I was watching, I noticed that the footage of both reports was from the same location and all that was different was the angle of the camera when the footage was taken.

The truth was obscured by political agenda. Remember, this took place before the advent of cellphones, yet the confusion, manipulation, distortion, escalating of emotions and polarizing of the community into volatile behavior was still present.

Gossip, fake news, hidden agendas are all attempts to derail us from our Divine Assignment.

Again, you will be vulnerable to these tactics IF you are not in tune with the Spirit of God and knowledgeable of the Word of God.

Nehemiah knew the secret plans of false friends.

I believe he received revelation knowledge regarding their plans.

We knew our enemies' intent was to intimidate us into stopping our work. They reasoned, "*These Jews will stop rebuilding out of fear and discouragement. Progress will grind to a halt.* " *Instead I renewed my dedication, strengthened my hands.*" Neh 6:9 Voice

All because Nehemiah was in tune with God, he became aware, enlightened and protected.

3) Religious Distraction

Later I went to visit Shemaiah son of Delaiah and grandson of Mehetabel, who was confined to his home. He said, "Let us meet together inside the Temple of God and bolt the doors shut. Your enemies are coming to kill you to-night. "

But I replied, "Should someone in my position run from danger? Should someone in my position enter the

Temple to save his life? No, I won't do it!"

I realized that God had not spoken to him, but that he had uttered this prophecy against me because Tobiah and Sanballat had hired him. They were hoping to intimidate me and make me sin. Then they would be able to accuse and dis-credit me.

Remember, O my God, all the evil things that Tobiah and Sanballat have done. And re-member Noadiah the prophet and all the prophets like her who have tried to intim-idate me. Neh. 6:10-14

ARK Angels are not called to hide under the protective disguise of religion!

Nehemiah was an ARK Angel for his time.

- Advancement not retreat;
- Fulfilling the call, not self-protection (IF he would have been tricked into the self-protection trap, they were go-ing to use it to destroy his reputation and thus the protection from the King.); and
- Victory minded not victim thinking.

Principle of the Hearing Ear

Many advisors and strategies may sound logical and reasonable, yet in order to be protected, one MUST be in direct intimate communication with the Holy Spirit!

Vulnerability to human wisdom and the Babylonian system will lead you down the wrong path where a snare will be waiting for you!

Nehemiah's response was consistent. It was **FOCUS** on his Divine Assignment, period!

Nehemiah's Message***: I am in the middle of a great work and cannot be interrupted. I am not coming down to meet with you. What is so important that I should suspend this great work we are doing to travel to see you?***

"*I'm in the middle of a Great Work*" or "*I am in the middle of accomplishing my Divine Assignment*" or "*I am in the middle of seeing my PURPOSE come to completion*" are the proper responses you should have when faced with seemingly genuine invitations to follow any path other than your Divine Assignment!

Whatever you say about your obstacles, remember that there is nothing these distracting voices have to say to you that is more important than your Call from God!

ARK Angels will NEVER negotiate with the enemy!

It is the benign believer that will.

A benign tumor is a mass of cells (tumor) that lacks the ability to invade neighboring tissue or metastasize. Not a threat.

Pathology: Not malignant; is self-limiting; not a threat.

Syn. Not progressive, harmless, accommodating. Benign believers do not grow or take territory. They just appear to be something.

Benign believers will NEVER be ARK Angels, Kingdom Builders or Victorious Saints!

Let me tell you a story about Chris. His parents named him Christian but everyone called him Chris for short. One day, Chris was driving his car for a fairly long distance when he saw a hitchhiker. Chris picked up the hitchhiker because he felt sorry for him. Chris and the passenger were having a good conversation and Chris was becoming more and more relaxed with the hitchhiker. Chris had to stop for gas and after the gas stop, Chris invited the hitchhiker to sit in the front seat instead of the backseat. Chris believed that that would create better conversation. Chris is getting closer to his destination and he is excited and dreaming of the great reunion with friends and family.

Suddenly, the hitchhiker grabs the steering wheel yanks it and Chris and the cargo propelling into a ravine. The car is a mangled wreck and yet Chris survives. He is not in very good shape. As a matter fact, he has broken bones and internal injuries. In his delirium, he vaguely sees the hitchhiker walking happily away from the crash.

This brief story is a parable. So what does this parable mean?

Chris represents every Christian.

The vehicle represents their Divine assignment, and purpose.

The hitchhiker represents the enemy of our soul, worldly belief systems and/or emotions.

The location of the hitchhiker reveals the Christian's lack of awareness. At first, the hitchhiker is at the side of the road.

Chris, the Christian, sees the hitchhiker and feels sorry for him. Chris, the Christian, allows his emotions to make his decisions for him.

Now the hitchhiker is in the backseat of the car building rapport with Chris, the Christian. Over time a comfort zone is created. The hitchhiker is invited to the front seat, right beside the driver.

And he is now in a position to seize control over the vehicle (the Christian's Divine Assignment and Purpose).

The ravine represents the damage and the consequences that are a result of getting comfortable with this stranger you have invited into your purpose.

Don't compromise what God has told you to do!

Don't make a peace treaty with the enemy – Satan, culture, humanism or your soulish desires!

Whatever God has for your life (Heavenly Purpose, Divine Assignment and Spiritual Gifting), give yourself to it and you'll come up blessed every time!

Do you think that the enemy of your soul will leave you alone if you leave him alone? Just because you make a peace treaty with him doesn't mean you'll have peace. Remember, he is a covenant breaker, traitor, and father of lies!

Don't get fooled into destruction!

ARK Angel Manifesto

ARK Angels need to turn their Hearing Ear to the Voice of the Spirit of God!

Courage, not compromise, brings the smile of God's approval.

Thomas S. Monson

Compromise makes a good umbrella, but a poor roof

James Russell Lowell

Chapter Seventeen

Faithfulness of an ARK Angel

Noah was faithful! If he had not been faithful, he would not have entered the ark. Being faithful doesn't mean that you started well; it means that you finished well.

Websters defines "faithful" this way:

Definition of **faithful**. 1: full of faith. 2: steadfast in affection or allegiance 3: true to the facts, to a standard, or to an original.

1.Faithful means being FULL of FAITH! Faithfulness means meta-physical.

Now faith is the assurance (title deed, confirmation) of things hoped for (divinely guaranteed), and the evidence of things not seen [the conviction of their reality—faith comprehends as fact what cannot be experienced by the physical senses]. Hebrews 11:1 (AMP)

Therefore, Faithful means we are SO FULL of Hebrews 11:1, so that we are able to consistently commit to the UNSEEN reality of our Divine Assignment!

2.Steadfast in affection and allegiance

Faithfulness is relationship. This cannot happen without a personal relationship. So being faithful means the roller-coaster of emotions are obliterated and replaced with unwavering affection and allegiance.

3.True to the facts, to a standard, or to an original Faithfulness is alignment.

When you are faithful, you are aligned to the Truth. Noah was aligned to the Word he received from God. If we are to be faithful to our assignment, we need to be aligned to the WORD of GOD.

When you are faithful, you are aligned to a standard. Noah aligned himself to the standard of the divine construction plan that God gave him. Otherwise, the ark would have sunk! If we are to be faithful, we also need to align ourselves to the standard of the WORD of GOD. If a team member is to be faithful to their team, they must align themselves to the standard the coach has set before them. If you are to be faithful at your place of employment, you must align your behavior and activity to the standard set forth by the employer.

When you are faithful you are aligned to the original. Noah aligned himself to the original plan for humanity while the world went totally out of alignment with God's original plan. Remember, we are created in the image of God. Adam and Eve were the originals. They got out of alignment. Jesus Christ came to create the opportunity for us to regain our alignment to the original. He became the last Adam and purchased the original identity for all who believe through his sacrifice for our sins (our misalignment) and resurrection! Through Christ our original identity has been restored.

Therefore, we are faithful when we consistently align ourselves to this new identity! The great thing about alignment is that there is less friction, greater functionality and less wear and tear when properly aligned!

When you are aligned to the WORD of GOD, the WILL of GOD, and the CALLING of GOD, there will be less friction, turmoil and wear and tear on your soul (your emotions and your mind). There will be clarity instead of confusion.

When I was sixteen, I bought a car from a neighbor. He wanted to get rid of it because it was costing him too much to drive it. So I bought it for $600. 00. According to my neighbor the problem with the car was that it was causing the tires to wear out every 3-6 months. This was costing him a lot. He had many people look at the car to determine the problem but they could not solve it.

So I bought it by FAITH. I was believing in an UNSEEN solution and my hope in finding it was firmly anchored. I brought the car home with the new tires that my neighbor had just installed. I started tinkering and looking. I am not a mechanic even in the most liberal of definitions. My dad thought I had just wasted $600. 00 because he knew the neighbor and trusted him. As I was looking rather unintelligently at the motor and car, a thought POPPED into my head. It was ridiculous.

It only required faith and a screwdriver.

I acted by faith and used the screwdriver. I began to drive the car and check the tires periodically. I drove that car for more than two years without needing to change the tires! I then sold it to my mechanic cousin for more than I had initially paid for it! I did not invest in tires, auto parts or auto repair manuals.

I just used what was in my hand – a screwdriver!

God asked Moses what was in his hand and his Divine Assignment was birthed.

God is asking you what is in your hand (in your possession or within you) and God's divine assignment for you will be birthed!

Let's sum up faithfulness.

Faithfulness is being FULL of confident belief in the Character and Calling of God resulting in unwavering affection and allegiance while actively staying in alignment with Divine Truth, godly standards and your original design.

Or "to do what you are supposed to do, when you are supposed to do it whether you feel like it or not"

Faithfulness is rewarded!

The reward of faithfulness is JOY, RESPECT, PEACE, INCREASE, & BLESSINGS!

ARK Angel Manifesto

"For to everyone who has [and values his blessings and gifts from God, and has used them wisely], more will be given, and [he will be richly supplied so that] he will have an abundance" Matthew 25:29a AMP

Principle of Faithfulness

The reward of Faithfulness is an ABUNDANCE of Fruitfulness!

Unfaithfulness is also rewarded!

"But from the one who does not have [because he has ignored or disregarded his blessings and gifts from God], even what he does have will be taken away." Matthew 25:29b AMP

Principle of Unfaithfulness

The reward for Unfaithfulness is ABUNDANCE of Barrenness!

Faithfulness and Unfaithfulness are equally rewarded with ABUNDANCE but *always after their own kind*. It's the *Multiplication of SEED Principle!*

This principle goes directly against the welfare mentality.

Expectation without seed produces an empty harvest of futility.

When you are faithful, God will honor you with two things:

1. Increase in that specific area of faithfulness
2. Increase your ABILITY to Expand your areas of Influence and Stewardship

If people would realize that it is through faithfulness that God blesses their life would be fewer people crying for hand-outs and more people actively advancing the Kingdom through fulfilling their Divine Assignment!

"A faithful man will abound with blessings"

Prov. 2:20 NKJV

This is a promise of God!

This is a recipe of REWARD!

God doesn't reward talent.

God doesn't reward good intentions.

God doesn't reward Church membership.

God rewards faithfulness especially faithfulness to your Divine Assignment.

I think I need to clarify something very important here before we continue! Many people, including myself, could easily get the condemning voice in our spirit reminding us of how unfaithful we have been. Therefore, we need to remember that

FAITHFULNESS does not mean PERFECTION!

Our hearts and conscience will remind us of that continuously. But here is the good news!

"Even though our inner thoughts may condemn us with storms of guilt and constant reminders of our failures, we can know in our hearts that God Himself is ***greater*** *than any accusation.* ***He knows all things.****" 1 John 3:20 Voice*

- He knows we are a new creation.
- He knows that we are justified and made righteous.
- He knows we are "Blessed with every spiritual blessing in the heavenly realms in Christ Jesus"
- He knows we are forgiven.
- He knows that we are loved with an everlasting love.
- He knows we are a royal priesthood.
- He knows we are holy and full of grace.
- He knows that we are more than conquerors.
- He knows that we are His child.
- He knows that we are the head and not the tail.
- He knows that we are significant and secure in our relationship with Him.

It is this knowledge of us that surpasses any accusation or condemnation that comes from our heart! Yes God is greater than our hearts! Isn't that AMAZING? As we renew our minds, we too will know these truths as well!

Back to Noah. I do not believe that Noah

- Measured every board perfectly,

- Always hit the "nail" on the head (sometimes it was the thumb)
- Was always positive and optimistic when he faced the annoying pressure of foolish unbelief continually attacking him.
- Was perfectly patient with his children and a perfect parent.

I do believe that Noah had flaws! Amidst his flaws, his faith remained his anchoring point. His relationship with God remained connected. Therefore, be encouraged. You are not disqualified by your past, your failures or your weaknesses.

Therefore . . .

Awaken your faith!

Restore your intimacy with Christ!

Re-energize your passion for the Word of God! Resurrect your Divine Assignment from the rubble of your past!

There may be detours, distractions, discouragement and defeat along the way; and yet you can stay in faith and make it your foundation!

Stay connected to the Author and Finisher of your faith!

Faith is the journey of *implementation*!

It's about **progress**, **growth**, change of **heart beliefs**, and learning **life lessons** that **propel** you into the ***Arms of Grace***!

There was this pastor of a medium sized congregation.

He preached a powerful message one Sunday morning. It came from his heart and the WORD of GOD. In essence, he was revealing the heart of God to the congregation.

The next Sunday, he preached the exact same message. A few of the people commented to each other about this. They chalked it up to the pastor forgetting he had preached it the week before.

The third Sunday comes around and, yes, you guessed it, he preached the exact same message once again!

At this point many in the congregation knew there was a problem and approached the elders. They asked the elders to talk with the pastor about this matter. A few congregants even told the elders that they refuse to pay a pastor who merely repeats the same sermon week in and week out.

The elders approach the pastor and shared their concerns.

The pastor listened carefully and respectfully. Then he replied,

"Friends, I appreciate your concerns. I would like to let you know that I knowingly preached the same message for three Sundays in a row. It was not a mistake or oversight.

Many people in the congregation didn't even realize that it was the same message three weeks in a row. Those that did notice complained that they did not appreciate my laziness in sermon preparation.

So here is the truth: The Lord has given me many messages to share with this congregation.

I am not short of material.

But I will continue preaching this message until this congregation will actively implement it into their lives through obedience and faith.

What good would it be for me to preach a new sermon next week when this one was not planted in fertile ground?

If you are desiring a fresh Word from God, make sure that you are faithfully applying the last word you received!

Faith is a VERB! As the disciple James clearly teaches in James 2:17, ***"so then faith that doesn't involve action is phony"*** TPT.

The same is true with faith. Without actions, faith is useless. By itself, *it's* as good as *dead.* Voice

---

Just as Noah faithfully implemented the call of God for his life, God is looking for ARK Angels in the 21th century who will faithfully answer the call to build an Ark of Hope, Peace and Deliverance in a Turbulent World!

Faith is not the power of positive thinking; it is believing in God and trusting that His Will and Word is always best even when you cannot understand why.

Shari Howerton, Breaking the Chains

Chapter Eighteen

FAITH – the Heartbeat of an ARK Angel

By faith, Noah . . ."

It does not say "by effort", "by teamwork", "by good intentions", or "by the sweat of his brow".

It's by faith!

Many people have criticized the ***Faith Movement***. Many have declared that the Faith Movement is dead and gone. Many have even accused the Faith Movement of destroying the integrity of the Church.

"By **faith**, Noah . . . prepared an ark!

First of all, the Faith Movement is not a movement!

Bowels have movements, FAITH doesn't.

Secondly, Faith is a lifestyle. It is how you live. It is the fountain from which your thoughts, attitudes, decisions and behavior manifest.

Thirdly, Faith is the ONLY way we please God!

Therefore, if the Faith "Movement" is gone so is our ability to please God!

Hebrews 11:6 tells us that **"without faith, it's impossible to please God"**

Everything that we do that pleases God originated from FAITH! If the action's origin is not faith, no matter how well you do it and no matter how spiritual you look while doing it; **it does not please God!**

Believers, do you want to please God? Then you will have to embrace the ***Lifestyle of Faith***.

Faith is not a feeling, emotion or idea! It is even more than a lifestyle. It is a LOCATION! In the Greek the word "without" comes from the Greek word "*choris*". *Choris* means to be outside of something, such as someone who lives outside the perimeter of a city. It reflects the contrast between being inside and outside something such as ***in*** the house or ***out*** of the house. Therefore, *choris* depicts someone who is *out of,* not *in,* a specific location.

Faith therefore is a location. This location represents your relationship to God the Father, Son (Jesus Christ) and Holy Spirit. It also represents your Divine Assignment! It also represents **the Kingdom of God within us**! Like the saying goes, "Location, Location, Location!"

> *"When you live outside of faith – venturing, exploring, visiting or residing beyond the boundaries and perimeters of Faith – you make it impossible to please Him"* Heb. 11:6

Inside the boundaries and perimeters of Faith is where your Divine Assignment is located.

If you really want to discover if you are *inside* or *outside* of Faith, ask yourself the following questions:

1. Am I doing what God has revealed for me to do?

2. Am I fulfilling the assignment He gave for my life?
3. Am I living in obedience to His WORD and to the REVELATION He has given me?
4. Am I consistently staying FIXED on my Purpose in thought, attitude and actions?

REALITY CHECK

If you say, "Well, I "**tried"** that faith stuff and it didn't work." I suggest that you stop doing the devil's work for him! He has been "**trying"** people's faith from the beginning of time. We are not to "**try**" our faith but rather as Hebrews 10:38 tells us that "the righteous will live by faith". Faith is not an experiment, it is a LIFESTYLE! ***Faith is a universal law.***

So you see, faith by itself isn't enough. Unless it produces good deeds, it is dead and useless.

Now someone may argue, "Some people have faith; others have good deeds." But I say, "How can you show me your faith if you don't have good deeds? I will show you my faith by my good deeds." James 2:18 NLT

The verse prior to this makes it very clear when it says, *"So then faith that doesn't involve action is phony."* TPT

Noah's faith was not phony! Noah showed his faith by his deeds and so do ARK Angels!

A number of years ago, I gave an analogy in the sermon I was preaching. I will share it here because I believe that it will clarify faith as a verb.

"Friends, please help me out by using your imagination. Imagine that as I am preaching this message, an usher walks up the aisle with a very somber face and a piece of paper in his hands. He hands me the note and disappears out the back. I silently read the note and a very serious look comes over my face. My sermon has been interrupted. I look up and say 'My dear congregation, let me read the note that was given to me: ***"I hate Christians and I have placed a bomb in your Church that will detonate at 11:50 AM!"***

Friends, what's your reaction to this scenario?

Whatever your reaction is, it is totally based on faith.

If you promptly get up and leave, you have faith that the note is real.

If you remain seated, you have faith that the note is false.

Are you living at the address of Faith? Or have you moved out of Faith and into the neighborhood of doubt, fear and unbelief, where you know that you are no longer pleasing God?

Faith always demands ACTION! For example, if you have faith that the chair you are about to sit on, is not strong enough to hold your weight, you will refrain from sitting down.

This reminds me of an event that occurred in the mid-1850's

> Charles Blondin's greatest fame when he became the first person to cross a tightrope stretched 1,100 feet across the mighty Niagara Falls. People from both Canada and America came from miles away to see this great feat.
>
> He walked across, 160 feet above the falls, several times... each time with a different daring feat - once in a sack, on stilts, on a bicycle, in the dark, and blindfolded. One time he even carried a stove and cooked an omelet in the middle of the rope!
>
> A large crowd gathered and the buzz of excitement ran along both sides of the river bank. The crowd "Oohed and Aahed!" as Blondin carefully walked across - one dangerous step after another - pushing a wheelbarrow holding a sack of potatoes.
>
> Then a one point, he asked for the participation of a volunteer. Upon reaching the other side, the crowd's applause was louder than the roar of the falls!
>
> Blondin suddenly stopped and addressed his audience: *"Do you believe I can carry a person across in this wheelbarrow?"*

The crowd enthusiastically yelled, "**Yes**! You are the greatest tightrope walker in the world. **We believe!**"

"Okay," said Blondin, "***Who will get into the wheel-barrow."***

As far as the Blondin story goes, no one did at the time!

This unique story illustrates a real life picture of what faith actually is. The crowd watched these daring feats. They said they believed. But... their actions proved they truly did not believe. It's like us reading about the miracles recorded in the Bible, or we just happen to come across John 14:12 where it says,

"I tell you this timeless truth: The person who follows me in faith, believing in me, will do the same mighty miracles that I do—even greater miracles than these because I go to be with my Father! TPT

Or as the Amplified Translation translates it

I assure you and *most solemnly say to you, anyone who believes in Me [as Savior] will also do the things that I do; and he will do even greater things than these [in extent and outreach], because I am going to the Father.*

Now the question we must ask according to Blondin is, "***Who will get into the wheelbarrow."***

Noah's faith demanded action.

Your faith and my faith also demands action. If you don't act, then that is evidence that it is not part of your "FAITH Fabric". It means that you have wandered beyond the boundaries of Faith.

Like I mentioned before, Faith is not a movement.

Therefore, it is not a movement whose time has come and gone.

FAITH is still the message of the Church because God is still longing to be pleased.

I want to please God and I'm sure you do as well or you would not be reading this book. The way you'll please God is living by faith.

Did Noah overcome the world? YES, the world drowned but Noah stayed afloat and overcame the world! How did he do it? By building a boat? NO! According to Hebrews 11, it was by FAITH! Now let's fast forward to the New Covenant and our present day.

1 John 5:4-5 tells us that our victory over the world is also through FAITH!

*For everyone born of God is victorious and overcomes the world; and this is the victory that has conquered and overcome the world—**our [continuing, persistent] faith** [in Jesus the Son of God]. Who is the one who is victorious and overcomes the world? It is the one who believes and recognizes the fact that Jesus is the Son of God. (AMP)*

The NLT explains the power of overcoming faith this way:

*For every child of God defeats this evil world, and we achieve this victory through **our faith**. And who can win this battle against the world? **Only those** who believe that Jesus is the Son of God. (NLT)*

Just as Noah overcame the world through (continuing, persistent) faith, so also will you according to the **New Covenant Principle of Victory**!

ARK Angels, you are warriors and kingdom builders by FAITH!

- By **faith** you build and by **faith** you warn.
- By **faith** you take territory and by **faith** you protect your heart.
- By **faith** you receive revelation knowledge and by **faith** you vanquish doubt.
- By **faith** you speak life into dry bone situations and by **faith** you break the curses of the past.

■ By **faith** you think using the mind of Christ and by **faith** you take EVERY thought captive making it submit to the WORD of GOD.

*We are **demolishing** arguments and ideas, every high-and-mighty philosophy that pits itself against the knowledge of the one true God. We are **taking prisoners** of every **thought**, every **emotion**, and **subduing** them into **obedience** to the Anointed One. 2 Cor. 10:5 (Voice)*

■ By **faith** we see dreams and visions and by **faith** we bring them to reality.

■ By **faith** we share the Good News of Salvation and by **faith** we train disciples in righteousness.

Faith was the tool that Noah used to build the ark. Yes, faith is a tool.

As we all know, the hammer is a tool. A hammer can be used to build or to break something.

The same with faith. We can use it to build the Kingdom of God, take hold of God's promises and build a healthy marriage. We can also use the tool of faith for selfish ungodly things and break the manifestation of the BLESSING, ANOINTING and your DIVINE ASSIGNMENT that God has richly given you in Christ.

Just like a body can suffer from an infection that over time will begin to fester; our world is infected with fear and this festering fear needs the antiseptic of FAITH to be applied to their woundedness.

ARK Angel Manifesto

We are the nurse practitioners employed by the Great Physician! The WORD of GOD is the antiseptic that needs to be applied. Let's rise up and be the *ARK Angels of Healing!*

ARK Angels, I decree to you that it is time to get serious about BUILDING the ARK! The Church needs you to RISE UP! The world around you needs you to SPEAK UP! And the faith within you needs you to GROW UP!

It's time to use our faith in the WORD of GOD to build an Ark of Hope, Peace and Deliverance in a Turbulent World!

"Then the master told his servant, 'Go to the roads and paths! Urge the people to come to my house. I want it to be full. Luke 14:23 GW

Chapter Nineteen

ARK Angels Populate the ARK

BUILDING an Ark is great but populating the Ark is PARAMOUNT!

The Ark's purpose is not to celebrate the building genius of Noah in some museum somewhere; **it is to bring deliverance**.

ARK Angels, I believe that God has called you to rise up and prepare the Church to become an instrument of much salvation! The harvest is coming. Many around us are confused, even within the Church. Many are wounded in their soul.

Bodies are failing, Hope is falling, and Anger is fueling the storms within the lives of those around us.

ARK Angels, lift your hands to the sky with a heart full of Praise! God is the Answer! One reason why people raise their hands is because they have the answer. You all can recall that keener is school who whenever the teacher would ask a question, their hand immediately jumped to the sky.

So ARK Angels, raise up your hands and declare to the world that you have the answer!

Technology and rapid change is creating unmanageable stress and pressure in people's lives. People believe that there are no answers to their condition or even their world. They are looking for a simpler life, a solid foundation, genuine enjoyment, inner peace and security.

Nostalgia cannot give that to them. Yet many wish for the good old days to return, believing that it will result in the longings of their heart being fulfilled.

The hurting, hopeless and clueless among us are longing for answers. We have the answers because we have Christ **in us** and He is the ANSWER for the world today!

ARK Angels, it is time to build an Ark of answers for our confused culture.

- We have the answer to loneliness – Fellowship
- We have the answer to fear – God's unconditional love
- We have the answer to insecurity – We're called **by name** for a PURPOSE
- We have the answer to defeat – God's Armor
- We have the answer to inadequacy – God's Abundance
- We have the answer to every need – God's WORD

ARK Angels, time to raise our voice to the dry bones of defeated, discouraged and dead dreams; and once again SPEAK LIFE to them!

Remember the account of Moses, where God's people were delivered out of Egypt? They crossed the Red Sea and were free. Instantly they were out of Egypt and yet it took 40 years for them to get Egypt out of them! Egypt represents the carnal humanistic thinking and philosophies of the world.

When we stand up and declare that we have the answer, we are automatically also declaring that the world doesn't!

We do not need to go to the world for our answers.

They will **always be insufficient and inadequate**. We need to flee surface answers of the world because we possess the SUPERNATURAL answers of the WORD of GOD!

The "Egyptian" mindset is a cancer that has been malignant within the Body of Christ (Church) for too long!

The last chapter, you were reminded to take every thought captive to the obedience of Christ. This means there is NO ROOM for the worldly philosophies in the minds of ARK Angels!

We cannot mingle the WORD of GOD with the culture of the Father of Lies.

Instead, they mingled among the pagans and adopted their evil customs. Ps. 106:35 NLT

But mingled themselves with the [idolatrous] nations and learned their ways and works. Ps. 106:35 AMPC

ARK Angels do not mingle with the ways, works, customs, language or values of the world!

In Leviticus there is an account of "strange fire"! I believe that this strange fire was a mingling of God's instructions and their personal ideas.

Lee Grady (editor of Charisma Magazine) helps us as ARK Angels, disciples and Christ followers to guard ourselves against **strange fire**!

Below are excerpts of an article written by Lee Grady, warning the contemporary Church of embracing strange fire because they WILL GET BURNT!

> *"We need to be careful. Current fads involving angels, ecstatic worship and necromancy could push us off the edge of spiritual sanity.*
>
> *No one fully understands what Nadab and Abihu did to prompt God to strike them dead in the sanctuary of Israel. The Bible says they loaded their firepans with incense, ignited the substance and "offered strange fire before the Lord, which He had not commanded them" (Lev. 10:1, NASB). As a result of their careless and irreverent behavior, fire came from God's presence and consumed them.*
>
> ***Zap. In an instant they were ashes.***
>
> *"We want the miracles of God, but we also want the fear and reverence of God.* ***We cannot allow this strange fire to spread unchecked.*** *"*
>
> *This ancient story has relevant application for us today.*

We don't use incense or firepans in our worship, but we are expected to handle God's Word with care and minister to His people in the fear of the Lord. In other words: No funny business allowed. We aren't allowed to mix God's Word with foreign concepts or mix our worship with pagan practices.

Yet as I minister in various Churches around this country I am finding that strange fire is spreading in our midst-even in Churches that call themselves "Spirit-filled." Pastors and leaders need to be aware of these trends:

1. **Deadly visitations**. *In some charismatic circles today, people are claiming to have spiritual experiences that involve communication with the dead. One Michigan pastor told me last week that some Church leaders he knows promote this bizarre practice and base it on Jesus' experience on the Mount of Transfiguration. The logic is that since Jesus talked to Moses and Elijah on the day He was glorified, this gives us permission to talk to dead Christians and our dead relatives.*

Although little is said about these experiences from the pulpit (since the average believer is not ready to handle this "new revelation"), people in some streams of the prophetic movement are claiming to have visitations from Aimee Semple McPherson, William Branham, John Wimber or various Bible characters. And we are expected to say, "Ooooooo, that's so deep"-and then go looking for our own mystical, beyond-the-grave epiphany.

That is creepy. Communication with the dead was strictly forbidden in the Old Testament (see Deut. 18:11), and there is nothing in the New that indicates the rules were changed. **Those who seek counsel from the dead-whether through mediums and séances or in "prophetic visions"- are taking a dangerous step toward demonization.**

2. **Ecstatic rapture.** *Not long after ecstasy became known as a recreational drug, someone in our movement got the bright idea to promote spiritual ecstasy as a form of legitimate worship. The concept evolved from "spiritual drunkenness" to the current fad in which people gather at Church altars and pretend to shoot needles in their arms for a "spiritual high." Some preachers today are encouraging people to "toke the Holy Ghost"-a reference to smoking marijuana.*

I hate to be a party pooper, but the Bible warns us to "be of sound judgment and sober spirit" (1 Pet. 4:7).

There is plenty of freedom and joy in the Holy Spirit*; we don't have to quench it by introducing people to pagan revelry. Christian worship is not about losing control. Those who worship Jesus do it "in spirit and in truth" (John 4:24), and our love for God is not measured by how violently we shake or how many times we fall on the floor.*

3. **Angels among us**. *Angels have always played a vital role in the life of the Church. They are "ministering spirits" sent to protect, guide and strengthen believers (Heb. 1:14). But suddenly angels have become the rage in some segments of our movement. People are claiming to see them everywhere, and often the stories don't line up with the Word of God.*

I know God can do anything. He can make an iron axe head float, hide a coin in a fish's mouth and use a little boy's lunch to feed a multitude. Those were genuine miracles that He can still do today. But we still have to use caution here. There are counterfeits.

If we promote a false miracle or a false angel in the Lord's house, we are participating in strange fire. *I know of a case where a man was caught planting fake jewels on the floor of a Church. He told his friends he was "seeding the room" to lift the people's faith. I know of others who have been caught putting gold glitter on themselves in a restroom and then running back in a Church service, only to claim that God was blessing them with this special favor. Where is the fear of God when Christians would actually fabricate a miracle? This is a time for all true believers with backbones to draw clear lines between what is godly worship and what is pagan practice.*

We want the miracles of God, but we also want the fear and reverence of God. ***We cannot allow this strange fire to spread unchecked. "***

Now let's jump forward to Revelation 2:6, 14-15.

"But this is in your favor: You hate the evil deeds of the Nicolaitans, just as I do."

"But I have a few complaints against you. You tolerate some among you whose teaching is like that of Balaam, who showed Balak how to trip up the people of Israel. He taught them to sin by eating food offered to idols and by committing sexual sin. In a similar way, you have some of the Nicolaitans among you who follow the same teaching.

Have you ever wondered who the Nicolaitans were? Obviously they are practicing and promoting something that God really does not like! He actually HATES it!

The meaning of Nicolaitans in the Greek means ***"one who conquers and subdues the people"***. Early Church leaders inform us that the Nicolaitans were the spiritual descendants of Nicolas of Antioch. He was ordained as a deacon in Acts 6:5.

Everyone liked this idea, and they chose the following: Stephen (a man full of faith and the Holy Spirit), Philip, Procorus, Nicanor, Timon, Parmenas, and **Nicolas of Antioch (an earlier convert to the Jewish faith)**. (Italics mine)

Acts 6:5 tells us this Nicolas was "a proselyte of Antioch." The fact that he was a proselyte tells us that he was not born a Jew, but had converted from paganism to Judaism. Then he experienced a second conversion, this time turning from Judaism to Christianity. From this information, we know the following facts about Nicolas of Antioch:

• He came from paganism and had deep pagan roots, very much unlike the other six deacons who came from a pure Hebrew line. The pagan background of Nicolas meant that he had previously been immersed in the activities of the occult.

• He was not afraid of taking an opposing position, evidenced by his ability to change religions twice. Converting to Judaism would have estranged him from his pagan family and friends. It would seem to indicate that he was not impressed or concerned about the opinions of other people.

• He was a free thinker, and very open to embracing new ideas and concepts. Judaism was very different from the pagan and occult world in which he had been raised. For him to shift from paganism to Judaism reveals that he was very liberal in his thinking, for most pagans were actually very offended by Judaism. He was obviously not afraid to explore or embrace new ways of thinking.

• When he converted to Christianity, it was at least the second time he had converted from one religion to another. We don't know if, or how many times, he shifted from one form of paganism to another before he became a Jewish proselyte. His ability to easily change religious "hats" implies that he was not afraid to switch direction in midstream and go in a totally different direction.

According to the writings of the early church leaders, Nicholas taught a doctrine of compromise.

This doctrine did not believe it was essential for there to be total separation between Christianity and the practice of occult paganism. From early church records, it seems apparent that this Nicolas of Antioch was so immersed in occultism, Judaism, and Christianity, that he had an appetite for all of it.

He had no problem **INTERMINGLING** these belief systems in various concoctions and saw no reason why believers couldn't continue to fellowship with those still immersed in the black magic of the Roman Empire and its countless mystery cults.

Occultism was a major force waging war against the Early Church. In Ephesus, the primary pagan religion was the worship of Diana (Artemis). There were many other forms of idolatry in Ephesus, but this was the primary object of occult worship in that city.

In the city of Pergamos, there were numerous dark and sinister forms of occultism, making Pergamos one of the most wicked cities in the history of the ancient world.

In both of these cities, believers were attacked and persecuted fiercely by followers of the various pagan religions. Believers were forced to contend with paganism on a level far beyond all other cities.

It was very hard for believers to live separately from all the activities of paganism because paganism and its religions were the center of life in these two cities. Occult paganism was their **CULTURE**.

Slipping in and out of paganism would have been very easy for young or weak believers to do since most of their families and friends were still pagans. A converted Gentile would have found it very difficult to stay away from all pagan influences.

From early church history, we can see that the "doctrine" of the Nicolaitans was that it was all right to have one foot in both the pagan world and the Christian world. They also believed that one did not need to be so strict about separation from the world system in order to be a disciple of Christ.

This, in fact, was the doctrine of the Nicolaitans that Jesus "hated".

It led to a weak version of Christianity that was without power and without conviction – a defeated, worldly form of Christianity.

This kind of teaching would result in nothing but total defeat of its followers!

When believers allow sin and compromise to be in their lives, it drains away the power of the work of the Cross and the Power of the Spirit! The Power of the Cross and the Power of the Spirit were intended to be alive and living in a believers' life.

This is the reason the name Nicolas is so vital to this discussion. The evil fruit of the "doctrine" that Nicolas of Antioch preached and promoted, encouraged, worldly participation, leading people to actively indulge in sinful lifestyles and encouraged a lowering of the godly standard of the church.

In this way, he literally ***conquered the people***. As you are already well aware, compromise with the world belief system and dabbling in false religions,

---

ALWAYS results in a WEAKENED and POWERLESS form of Christianity!

And now fast forward to our present generation.

- How well are we doing at avoiding the mingling of Christianity and pagan practices?
- How well are we doing at discerning the truth of the Word of God and the subtle snares of other forms of spirituality?
- What is our opinion of the Nicolaitan Doctrine? Are we concerned about this doctrine? Do we see this doctrine as a threat to the Church of Christ?
- Do we know the Word of God well enough to even be able to separate truth from subtle errors?
- If the church that you attend was described in Revelation chapter 2, how would it be described?

ARK Angel Manifesto

In an age of relativity, the ABSOLUTES of God's Word are the ONLY answers that will anchor the soul and keep it from drifting and drowning!

You cannot trick believers into having more faith!

Deception, mingling, strange fire, convenient Christianity, compromise, trickery or false claims will NEVER elevate genuine faith and we cannot build the Ark of Deliverance with these materials!

Remember in the last chapter, you discovered that the only way to please God is through faith. Hebrews 11:1 tells us that "faith is the **SUBSTANCE** of things hoped for . . ."

This substance needs to include **solutions** – real, practical, God anointed solutions that turn questions into answers; pain into healing; despair into hope; sorrow into joy; defeat into victory; confusion into clarity; bondage into blessings; soul ties into freedom and the lost become found.

This faith must work in the real world and not merely create a feel good sermon or experience. It must contain substance!

Faith is not wishful thinking to help us feel good through a traumatic season in our lives; it is CONFIDENCE in the reality, authority and life changing POWER of the WORD of GOD!

ARK Angels, let's fill the Ark with divine answers, spiritual solutions and transformed lives!

This is NO TIME to Mingle with pagan practices or experiment with strange fire!

We cannot allow our previous humanistic training and thinking to remain in us!

We must grow to the place where that spiritually cancerous thinking is totally eradicated from us.

We must find ourselves no longer trusting in human methods, but totally trusting in God's ways.

That's what Noah did! He did not mingle the corruption of the culture around him with the revelation of God's will and God's ways!

If he had, **the Ark would have sunk**! Remember, the door on the Ark? It was shut and sealed by God!

It was a ***Door of Separation***!

A door that is not completely shut and sealed would let the waters of Judgement to come in! NO MINGLING ALLOWED!

ARK Angels fill the Ark with TRUTH! TRUTH is the Door of Separation. When Truth is embraced, it produces salvation, transformed lives and messengers of Truth.

ARK Angels build by the authority of Christ in them and the authority of the WORD of GOD!

Chapter Twenty

ARK Angels are Standard Bearers

> *But Noah found favor* and *grace in the eyes of the* LORD. *These are* the records of *the generations (family history) of Noah. Noah was a righteous man [one who was just and had right standing with God], blameless in his [evil] generation; Noah walked (lived) [in habitual fellowship] with God.* Gen. 6:8-9

Noah got God's attention! He was righteous. He was perfect in his generation. Perfect does not mean without any faults. Perfect refers to being mature. It means being complete in how God has designed the person. He was different than any other man in his generation!

God is attracted to different. God is always looking for men and women who possess that quality of being different. 2 Chronicles 16:9 says

---

"For the eyes of the Lord move to and fro throughout the earth that He may strongly support those whose heart is completely His."

God found that Noah was blameless in his generation, and God being committed to his Word, could not destroy Noah with the rest of the earth.

So Noah was perfect in his generation. In other words, he was mature; he walked responsibly. He lived connected to God.

God wants the Church to walk mature. That is why He needs ARK Angels to raise the standard - to be standard bearers not only for the watching world, but also for the Church at large.

God wants the Church to be blameless and mature in our generation, and he's given you and me the divine ability and authority to be that way! Ephesians tells us that God's Church will be holy, without spot or wrinkle, blameless, perfect in its generation.

You can be that mature, blameless body of Christ that the world will look at and say," my goodness, there's something different about them. They have hope in these days of darkness, when it looks like there is no hope. "

As a former schoolteacher, educator and counselor in a facility of incarcerated youth, and involved in various communities; I can tell you the people in the world are without genuine hope. Therefore, as the apostle Paul describes them as, *people without God and without hope in this life.*

The only ones that have anything going for them are the believers. Yet even within the Church, many Christians are suffering from hopelessness, and depression.

This is why we need ARK Angels to encourage the Christians that are weak in faith, weak in the Word and weak in intimacy with their Savior, in order to strengthen them so they can themselves be ARK Angels actively building the Kingdom of God!

All the time that Noah was building the ark, from day one to the last day of the hundredth year, two things were happening.

First, Noah was showing to the world that he trusted God over all the persecution, all the opposition, all the seduction; over everything that could come against him.

The second thing that was happening is that Noah brought judgment to the world. As ARK Angels, we also need to reflect the TRUTH so clearly that everyone is forced to make a choice. ARK Angels will see things actively happening as they build the Ark of the Kingdom of God. I believe God wants his Church to be a standard to a watching world. Just like Noah was a standard bearer to the corrupt world around him.

I really do not think that God wants his Church to be a judgmental, condemning or antagonizing Church. Rather, I believe God wants His Church to be a loving, prophetic, positive and culturally relevant Church that is actively inviting the world into an Ark of safety, security and solutions.

God wants us to be the standard.

The world needs to see something **different** in the Church.

They need to see some **real resurrection power**.

They need to see believers walking in their **divine authority**.

They need to see an **inner peace** that defies the generation they're living in.

They need to see **addicts delivered and set free**.

They need to see a true **harmony within diversity**, which will demonstrate the power of the love of Christ.

They need to see the **depressed find joy, the hopeless find purpose, the lost find direction and the confused find answers**.

The world needs to see **something**!!!They need to see an ark, something they can run to and say," I need help, PLEASE HELP ME!"

Not only the Church but also the world is realizing that the humanistic social programs are not working.

The Church needs to be standard bearers and raise the standard of the body of Christ in such a way that the world can look to the Church and realize there's hope – hope for their marriages, hope for their relationships, hope for their children, hope for security, hope for peace, hope for meaningful occupation and hope for an authentic life purpose!

The Church needs to be **involved** in society while still remaining blameless in this generation. Just like Noah was.

The Church needs to provide **answers**.

The Church is called to raise up the standard of **education**.

The Church is called to raise up the standard of ministry to the **homeless**.

The Church is called to raise up the standard of the **foster care system**.

The Church is called to raise up the standard of **equipping the unemployed.** Thus preparing them for meaningful employment where they are no longer below the poverty line but rather above the poverty line able to give back to their community.

The Church needs to raise the standard of **community leaders** who exemplify unity and harmony; not politically charged divisiveness.

The Church needs to raise the standard of their **marriages** so the world can see there is hope for theirs.

The Church is called to be standard bearers!

The Church needs ARK Angels to lead the way and equip the Church in being standard bearers for the watching world.

God is calling the church out of slumber, and to become wide-awake change agents.

The church is to influence every area of life. The idea of the Church sitting back and not getting involved in the earth is a heresy that has been around a long time. It's called Gnosticism, which teaches basically, that all "matter" is evil, and all spirit is good. This belief causes Christians to retreat from the world of conflicts and responsibility. It causes Christians to start thinking that the institutional Church is the **only manifestation** of God's Kingdom, so why bother to bring the principles of God's Kingdom into other areas of life.

This is a terribly sad belief system. It has been called "escape religion" and yet God calls it "salt that has become tasteless. "It is good for nothing anymore, so it is thrown out and trampled underfoot by men. When the church refuses to salt the earth, tyranny "**over"** the church will result!

ARK Angels are not only standard bearers, they are also authentic salt shakers!

God does not want us to try to escape the problems of life or to ignore them.

He wants us to take our faith and use it to turn around broken homes, broken marriages, and broken lives in a broken world!

I believe God wants the Church to be creative problem solvers and dynamic change agents. The same old isn't going to do it!

The confusing traditions of the past won't engage the hurting world! Religious ceremonialism and ritualism isn't working!

Trying to identify with the world by being like the world truly lacks the power and anointing of God! Yet many churches are attempting to entertain people into the Kingdom. This also is not working!

Noah had integrity and the Church needs to exemplify that type of integrity in this generation.

Creative solutions anointed by God are in great need!

Remember,

God is the ultimate in creativity because He is the CREATOR of the Universe! Therefore, since we are created in His image, we are created to be creative beings. Creative solutions are in our DNA. ***Now Church, let's be creative in turning our world to Jesus Christ!***

Like I mentioned earlier, the world is looking for ARK Angels to point the way to the Ark of hope, peace, and deliverance.

In reality, God longs for every believer to become an ARK Angel! Remember an ARK Angel is a standard bearer whose heart is totally Christ's and they're willing to count the cost of being His ambassador to the world. When you raise a godly standard and offer solutions, you are also by default making a judgment on the world's standard and ideas.

So how do you raise a godly standard?

First of all, we are to build the kind of life that influences every area of society and brings righteous judgment to every area of life. We are to judge every area of life with the standard of God's Word. Now here is where we have to be very careful because judgment can so easily slide into vindictive actions. When we raise a godly standard found on God's Word, it must be from a Heart of Love. We cannot tear down humanistic standards, if we don't have a righteous standard to present before them! Yes, God does want us to tear down the systems of the world, but only by presenting a standard that is actually better than theirs.

We do not tear down the world standards by belittling them, gossiping about them or just religiously dismissing them. We cannot raise a righteous standard through talk alone, we must offer a

---

Better Way with Better Methods, Better Solutions and Better Results.

Noah was a standard bearer to his generation. It was a time of great moral darkness. He stood as judgment to unrighteousness, because he demonstrated that it was possible to walk in the light. They invite judgement upon their moral degradation and darkness because Noah proved to them by his lifestyle that they also **could** obey God. Never, never, never do we have an excuse! How many of heard the following: "Well, you don't understand! Everybody's doing it!" Well, not everybody was doing it in Noah's time. There was somebody who wasn't doing it and that one who wasn't doing it judged the rest of them that were!

That's what God wants the Church to be.

I challenge you to show me a person who follows the" everybody is doing it" philosophy and become a GREAT leader or a GREAT success.

In Isaiah 60, God makes an invitation to His people.

"Arise, shine, for your light has broken through! The Eternal One's brilliance has dawned upon you. See truly; look carefully—darkness blankets the earth; people all over are cloaked in darkness. But God will rise and shine on you; the Eternal's bright glory will shine on you, a light for all to see. Nations north and south, peoples east and west, will be drawn to your light, will find purpose and direction by your light. In the radiance of your rising, you will enlighten the leaders of nations. " Is. 60:1-3 (Voice)

Arise! Shine! Your light has come; the LORD's glory has shone upon you. Though darkness covers the earth and gloom the nations, the LORD will shine upon you; God's glory will appear over you. Nations will come to your light and kings to your dawning radiance. CEB

The darker the perversion and corruption of the world becomes, the greater the churches opportunity is to shine brightly and bring judgment upon the systems of the world.

This won't happen automatically!

The church must arise! The church must shine! The church must wake up!

We must be reminded that everything required for us to display the glory of the Lord has already been given us –" the Lord's glory has shone upon you. "

As ARK Angels, you will be messengers of light, messengers of the glory of God, and messengers of divine solutions for destructive problems.

God has never told his people to be "societal hermits".

God has never even suggested that his people be intimidated by the evils of today's society. Actually, it's the opposite.

In the words of God to Joshua," **Be bold and courageous!"** We are called to stand against the sins of our nations and stand up for righteousness in our land.

As Christians we are to be separate people, and holiness. We are to lead different lifestyles than the world. We need to embrace a set of morals and beliefs that honor God.

But **NO!** Emphatically**, NO!** We must not run from or separate from society. We must become bright beacons of light, illuminating the path to the ***Ark of Deliverance!*** We must shine so bright that the distasteful nature and destructive consequences of the corrupted world will be clearly seen by those who are lost.

ARK Angel, this is your time to SHINE!

Chapter Twenty-One

ARK Angels are Next Gen Motivated

Why did Noah build the Ark?

In obedience to the Word of God and the motivation to preserve the next generation. He did it not only for himself but also for his children. It's all about legacy. If Noah had not got God's attention by his non compromising commitment to God, there would have been NO LEGACY!

As I studied the Genesis chapters related to the flood, I discovered that at the time when God told Noah to build the ark, he had no sons.

This means he already knew about the destruction of the world before we had children.

I look at many of the end time advocates and enthusiasts within the church today, who don't want to bring any children into this depraved and declining world.

They see it as protecting their children from persecution, rebellion and potentially turning their back against God. But if the end times are like the times of Noah, then the attitude of the church must be that of Noah's.

It must've taken great faith for Noah to even consider bringing children into a world that was destined to be destroyed in that generation.

This tells me that Noah was ***next generation motivated***. He knew that the only people to populate the New World were those inside the boat. So he had children. God gave Noah time to train up his children. They work beside their dad, they watched and they also saw the world getting worse and worse.

Yes, they did grow up in a corrupt society, but they also were learning righteousness by watching their dad and his relationship with God.

Noah sons did not receive a direct word from God to build an ark and they were not alive to hear God tell their dad to build it. Noah trusted God's Word, but Noah's children had to trust Noah's word.

They witnessed their father being mocked. As they grew older, they became part of a persecuted family.

Noah's family represented a distinct minority.

I'm sure that minorities today can understand the kind of persecution Noah's family must've experienced.

I have had a glimpse of the persecution of minorities myself.

When I was a teenager, my father worked in a northern community and brought his family with him.

Now the community was comprised of a majority of aboriginal people who had lived there for generations plus the Hydro construction population mandated to build Hydro dams and generator stations. When I went to school there, I made friends with everyone. The community had a community center which included curling rinks, hockey arena, bowling alley, and numerous other sports and recreational venues. I go there every day after school to play ping-pong. I was really quite good at ping-pong and so many people wanted to challenge me. One person, who was equally as good as me, was Randy Fidler.

On Fridays the entire Recreation Center was reserved for the aboriginal community. So, at seven o'clock on a Friday evening I was about to leave the recreation center. Randy says to me," Rob, why don't you join us and play indoor soccer in the arena?" Well, I said," Sure if I'm invited, I guess I can join. "This is where I observed a very valuable lesson.

As I was playing soccer with about 40 to 50 aboriginal youth, I realized that the rules were not exactly the same. There were times when they would push me off the ball and there be no penalty! I looked around to see if the ref was going to call anything. But he didn't. Even when he looked right at the offense, the whistle never blew. Then there was the time, when I tried to steal the ball from one of the other youth and I accidentally kicked his shin. Immediately the whistle blew!

So as a 14-year-old, I experienced the feeling of not having a voice. I experienced the emotion of injustice without any recourse.

Now this example is really a rather insignificant experience compared to the severe treatment of minorities around the world. But it gave me a glimpse of being powerless. It gave me a glimpse of having no voice. It gave me a glimpse of having to just except the abuse.

Noah's family got more than a glimpse!

And it doesn't matter if you're a majority or a minority.

What matters is - are you going to serve the purposes of God in your life and train up your children to be Godly seed?

For 100 years, they grew up with their father's vision from God growing up alongside them. They grew up watching their father sold out to God's vision. No matter what it cost him in comfort, compromise, or circumstance.

When Noah entered the ark, his wife, his three sons and their wives joined him. No. Remember, none of them ever received a direct revelation from God about the pending destruction of the world and the importance of building an ark.

Now this is amazing to me! I've had people share their revelation that God had given them and I saw their passion, I saw the conviction, I saw their excitement and I wanted to be excited with them. And yet it wasn't really real to me because I hadn't received or seen the vision myself. And yet Noah's family without a direct revelation from God's trusted Noah.

Another reason why this is so amazing to me is because his family had no reference point. There had never been rain. There is never been storms or floods. And they never heard of an Ark. Everything, about the vision that Noah shared with them was totally foreign. They could not relate to any of it in the physical realm. Noah was asking his family to join him on a journey into the totally unknown. And the amazing thing is, they did!

This is the mandate of today's ARK Angels. We also have to be ***next generation motivated.***

We are not here to build the ark for the past generation.

We are not here to build the ark only for our generation. We need to build the ark with our eyes fixed on the next generation!

Much of the problem with the church of today is that we have answers to questions this generation is not even asking.

We also seem to be clueless regarding the questions that they are asking. Maybe that is why 7out of 10 first year university or college students raised in a Christian home turn their back on God before the graduate.

We are not answering their questions! There are churches rising up that are seeking to communicate godly answers to the questions of this generation. They are becoming ARK Angels for our generation.

ARK Angels need to be like Noah.

We need to catch a revelation of our divine assignment and a clear vision of how to activate it in such a way that the next generation (the children of the church) will follow the Will of God and the Word of God, regardless of the mockery, pressure, persecution or temptation to compromise cascading against them. Talk about Noah's kids resisting peer pressure from all of their cousins or uncles or aunts. The neighboring kids all thought that they were idiots. Yet, they chose to follow their dad into the UNKNOWN.

This reminds me of a famous Aesop Fable. Let me share it with you.

A Man and his son were once going with their Donkey to market.

As they were walking along by its side, a countryman passed them and said: *"You fools, what is a Donkey for but to ride upon?"*

So the Man put the Boy on the Donkey and they went on their way.

But soon they passed a group of men, one of whom said: *"See that lazy youngster, he lets his father walk while he rides."*

So the Man ordered his Boy to get off, and got on himself.

But they hadn't gone far when they passed two women, one of whom said to the other: *"Shame on that lazy lout to let his poor little son trudge along."*

Well, the Man didn't know what to do, but at last he took his Boy up before him on the Donkey.

By this time they had come to the town, and the passers-by began to jeer and point at them.

The Man stopped and asked what they were scoffing at.

The men said: *"Aren't you ashamed of yourself for overloading that poor donkey of yours and your hulking son?"*

The Man and Boy got off and tried to think what to do.

They thought and they thought, till at last they cut down a pole, tied the donkey's feet to it, and raised the pole and the donkey to their shoulders.

They went along amid the laughter of all who met them till they came to Market Bridge, when the Donkey, getting one of his feet loose, kicked out and caused the Boy to drop his end of the pole.

In the struggle the Donkey fell over the bridge, and his fore-feet still being tied together he was drowned.

"That will teach you," said an old man who had followed them: *"Please all, and you will please none"*

What if Noah was like the man going to the market with his son? Humanity would have been like the donkey, ***we would have ALL drowned in our attempts to be free.***

What if Noah's sons would have listened to the jeers and criticisms of the passersby as they were helping their dad build the Ark or recruiting the animals for the Ark?

Church – there are all kinds of VOICES criticizing us and seeking to control us.

Just as in Noah's time, we the church must not listen to those VOICES but rather hear from God and stay focused on building the Ark of God's Kingdom! If like the man in the fable, we seek to please everyone, it will then be IMPOSSIBLE to PLEASE GOD!

In order for the ARK Angels of this generation to be effective, they need to understand the questions that their lost generation is struggling with.

Then ARK Angels need to discover answers and then clearly communicate those answers in a relevant and understandable manner founded firmly on the Word of God!

Noah was respected the most by those who knew him the best: his children and his wife.

ARK Angels have the same challenge. In too many cases, we are respected the most by those who know us the least. This does not result in impactful influence and loyal leadership. As a potential ARK Angels, you must look deep inside yourself and ask a very difficult question:

ARK Angel Manifesto

"Do those who really know me the best respect me the most?"

If the answer is "**no**", then you need to change something so that you can reverse the answer.

You will never bring the next generation into the Ark of Victory, if your internal integrity is in question by those who know you best.

ARK Angels are next generation motivated. Their character, values and beliefs are seeds that they plant in the soil of the next generation. Their character is a character of integrity. Their values reflect the heart of God. And their beliefs are founded on the Word of God.

A seed is the package of immeasurable potential!

Your lives are seeds planted into the lives of future generations. These seeds can be beautifully creative or demonically destructive.

Can you imagine a world where every parent chose to plant the seeds of integrity, the heart of God and the word of God into every one of their children? As I look back at my life, I wish that those who raised me and mentored me as a child would have been these kinds of seeds. And to be honest, I wish that I had been a better quality seed of integrity, compassion, and reflection of the Heart of God and the Word of God to my children! So, just as Noah was a seed of faith and righteousness to his children, ARK Angels are ***seeds of hope, peace and deliverance in a turbulent world!***

Chapter Twenty-Two

NOW Recruiting ARK Angels

This is the last chapter of ***ARK Angel Manifesto***. I have explained the events of the Great Flood and Noah's epic involvement in it! I described the culture during the time of Noah. Matthew chapter 24, reminds us that the Son of Man, Jesus Christ, will come again during a time that reflects the culture and attitude of the days of Noah.

I hope I convinced you that we are living in a time that is becoming more and more and more reflective of that time.

I also hope that I convinced you that turbulent times are here and the world needs a ***Noah Revolution*** – active ark builders to save as many people as are willing to enter the ARK of Deliverance!

I also described ark builders as people who are actively building the Kingdom of God. I taught that ark building and kingdom building are synonymous. Also, as ark builders, our vision and our activity is to flesh out the Lord's Prayer when it says ***"Thy Kingdom come on Earth as it is in heaven"***.

As you can see, this is a massive job. For the church of Jesus Christ to be successful and influential in bringing multitudes of people into the **Ark of Deliverance**, we need to recruit a massive army of dedicated ark builders.

We need ARK Angels!

ARK Angel Manifesto

This book is not just about information and describing the culture of corruption that we are living in, this book is also a recruitment manual. It is a ***MANIFESTO***! That is faith without works is dead. Therefore, we must take action. In order for us to initiate a successful ***Noah Revolution***, we need an army of ARK Angels!

Let me share a letter that was written many years ago and yet it captures the critical need of ARK Angels not merely church attenders, convenient Christians or status quo saints.

This letter to a Christian is from a friend who had embraced the Marxist philosophy for the world.

"And the gospel of Jesus Christ is a much more powerful weapon than is our Marxist doctrine. All the same, it is we, the Marxists, who will finally beat you. We are only a handful and you Christians are numbered in the millions. But if you remember the story of Gideon and his 300 companions, you will understand why I am right. We communists do not play with words. Of our salaries and wages, we keep only what is necessary and we give the rest for propaganda purposes. To this propaganda. We also concentrate all of our free time and a part of our holidays. You Christians, however, give only a little time and hardly any monies to the spread of the gospel of Christ. How can anyone believe in the supreme value of the gospel if you do not practice it? If you do not spread it? If you do not sacrifice either time or money for it? Believe me, it is we who will win. For we believe in our communist message and we are ready to sacrifice everything, even our lives. But you Christians are afraid to soil your hands. "

(Author unknown)

ARK Angel Manifesto

ARK Angels are much like the writer of this letter, but with one significant difference. They have the attitude and the passion of this writer, but their focus is on sharing their intimate, dynamic, life-changing relationship with Jesus Christ to those lost and hurting in a turbulent world. ARK Angels, see their Christianity not as a hobby or a philosophical preference but rather they see it as their EVERYTHING!

So with the attitude that the previous writer passionately attached to the Word of God and the Will of God, we declare the following ***ARK Angel Manifesto*** as our marching orders and chosen lifestyle:

In the Ark that Noah built, only eight people entered the Ark of Deliverance. As ARK Angels of the 21st century, let's fill the Ark! The Ark of Salvation; the Ark of Deliverance; and the Ark of Hope! Let's FILL the Ark – that's our mandate, that's our call, yes, that's our purpose!

---

*A **manifesto** is a published declaration of the intentions, motives, or views of the issuer which promotes a course of belief and behavior that the author prescribes as a solution*

We LOVE

✓ God and his Divine Purposes.

✓ All people and nations because they are the focus of God's Love, Compassion and Grace.

✓ Supernatural manifestations of God's interactive participation in the lives of the people He loves.

✓ Witnessing TRANSFORMED LIVES.

✓ Sharing GOOD NEWS.

✓ Being active partners with The Way, the Truth and the Abundant Life – aka Jesus Christ - *our Savior, our Lord and our coming King.*

✓ Operating in our Spiritual Gifts in order to Advance the *Kingdom of God.*

✓ *The Covenant Blessings of God.*

We believe in the

✓ Existence and power of God.

✓ Authority of the believer.

✓ Indwelling presence of the Holy Spirit.

✓ Resurrection power of Christ resident in every believer.

✓ ANOINTING that breaks every yoke.

✓ Fivefold ministry.

✓ Need of the Five-Fold Ministries to build an unsinkable Ark able to stay afloat in TURBULENT times.

✓ Creative power of the words we speak.

✓ Mandate of the Angels of God which is to serve God's people for divine purposes.

✓ Quickly approaching Day of ETERNAL glory for all who BELIEVE.

✓ World's desperate need for hearing a VOICE of Compassion, Love and Truth so they will know the way to the ARK of Deliverance.

✓ Fact that the VICTORY is already won.

✓ Mind of Christ being a dynamic possession of every believer.

✓ Sacrificial love of Christ and that it is MORE POWERFUL than the corruption of the world.

✓ DYNAMIC reality of true spiritual obedience. True spiritual obedience is ALWAYS GREATER in transformational power (to create hope, peace, purpose, deliverance and divine favor) than ANY amount of religious sacrifice and duty.

✓ Hope of the world resting in the believer's hands.

✓ Only way to please God is through FAITH!

✓ True architects of Noah's ARK were FAITH, HOPE and LOVE!

Therefore, as we grow in FAITH, HOPE and LOVE, we dramatically increase our effectiveness as ARK Angels!

✓ ARK half empty has NEVER been the desire of God!

Therefore, we are anointed to INVITE the lost not FIGHT them.

Our mandate is to light the way to the ARK not chase the lost deeper into their DARKNESS

✓ DIVINE ASSIGNMENT of EVERY BELIEVER!

✓ POWER of unity and fellowship!

- This unity will not compromise TRUTH in order to create a diluted, delusional and deceptive version of unity!

✓ Heartbeat of VICTORY resonates in every SEED of FAITH!

We are committed to

✓ Lifelong growth in our Covenant Relationship with Jesus Christ.

✓ Cultivating a Sensitive Spirit.

✓ Possessing a Listening Ear to the Heart of God.

✓ Hearing the Word of God with FAITH.

✓ Accepting God's Divine Assignment regardless of the Personal Cost.

✓ Gathering the people and resources needed to build an Ark of Hope and Deliverance.

✓ Fueling FAITH with Action.

✓ NEVER making the Approval of People our Priority.

✓ Growing in Discipline, Perseverance and Consistency.

✓ Following the footsteps of Jesus by increasing in wisdom, maturity, and in favor with God and people.

✓ Continually inviting people into the Ark of God's Kingdom instead of merely complaining about the corruption around us.

✓ Honoring our individual DIVINE ASSIGNMENT as an INTEGRAL part of the Body of Christ's MANDATE.

✓ Being ACTIVE Messengers of the ***Noah Revolution.***

I, ________________________ hereby AFFIRM the *ARK Angel Manifesto* as reflecting my spiritual heartbeat! I declare that I, ____________________ will embrace the ARK Angel Manifesto as the blueprint for my values, decisions and motivation in all that I choose to be involved in. I, ________________________, choose to enroll in the ***"Noah Revolution"*** as an active member, preacher of Righteousness and builder of the Ark of Deliverance.

________________________ ____________

Signature **Date**

In closing, I will BLESS every reader and ARK Angel with the words of Psalm 32:6-10

"Therefore, let all the godly pray to you while there is still time, that they may not drown in the flood-waters of judgment. For you (God) are my hiding place; you protect me from trouble. You surround me with songs of victory.

The Lord says, "I will guide you along the best pathway for your life. I will advise you and watch over you. Do not be like a senseless horse or mule that needs a bit and bridle to keep it under control. " Many sorrows come to the wicked, but unfailing love surrounds those who trust the LORD."

Since you have read, searched your heart and embraced the tenets of the ***ARK Angel Manifesto***, and signed your commitment to this powerful document, here is a Prayer and a Confession for you!

PRAYER of FAITH

Lord, help me stay loyal to the assignment You have given me as an ARK Angel. I know that is where I am supposed to be – and I know that is what I am supposed to be doing. Forgive me for vacillating back and forth, in and out of my Divine Assignment. I am asking You to help me become single-minded, concentrated, and focused in fulfilling my Divine Assignment never to wander out of Faith again. I want to live at the address of Faith, for I know that is where I will please You the most. Holy Spirit, empower me to push aside every distraction of the devil and to remain fixed and focused on doing exactly what God has instructed me to do.

I pray this in Jesus' name!

FAITH CONFESSION

I confess that I live "in" faith. Although Satan tries to use situations to distract me, dissuade me and detour me from staying in faith, I have resolved that I am never moving from the place where God has called me to be. I will never relinquish the dream He has lovingly placed in my heart. I will stay in this place; I will use my faith; I will be steadfast, unwavering, and committed to seeing His Promises manifested in my life. I will count the cost of fulfilling my Divine Assignment and I will see my Kingdom building project completed!

Because I have made this decision, I am a person who pleases God! I declare this by faith in Jesus' name!

Adapted from Rick Renner

ARK Angels, Your DIVINE ASSIGNMENT awaits your RISING UP because you have been called ***"For such a Time as This"!***

I BLESS every reader with ***increased Faith, supernatural Courage and undistracted Loyalty to your Divine Assignment!***

I speak LIFE into your ***dreams anointed by Holy Spirit!***

I speak a REVITALIZATION of ***Holy Spirit's involvement in your walk of Faith!***

I speak ***RESURRECTION POWER*** to saturate your obedience to your Divine Call!

I speak a ***DIVINE REFRESHING*** of JOY, PEACE, LOVE and BOLDNESS in your spirit!

I speak a ***renewal of HOPE*** and a ***release of the MESSAGE that God has birthed within you for the nations!***

I DECLARE your LIFESTYLE and MESSAGE will release ***LIFE, HOPE and DELIVERANCE*** to people drowning outside the ARK of the Kingdom of God!

I DECLARE that your FAITH will never suffer from **LARYNGITIS** but boldly and clearly speak of the GOODNESS and POWER of God for every need!

In Jesus' Name, I call it done! AMEN

About the Author

Robert Klassen, MA is the President of ***REFRESH Your LIFE, International.***

He is a Certified Speaker, Coach, Teacher & Trainer with the John Maxwell Team; an ordained minister, educator/counsellor for incarcerated youth, conference speaker and pastor.

Rob has experienced a wide variety of life experiences. He lived in 18 houses by the time he was 18 years old. From grade 1 to grade 12, he went to 10 different schools. His life was always changing – from city life to small-town life; from sub-arctic living to living on a farm; from a huge city school to a one room schoolhouse. Whenever he would get a close friend, it was time to move again. Sports was his ticket for entering the new world each new community presented. This created a limiting belief of ***Performance-Based Approval*** that held him in bondage for a very long time. It was the revelation of **LOVE-Based Approval** that transformed and continues to transform his life!

With this variety of experience, he has witnessed the deep needs of a hurting world. These deep needs also impacted his personal life creating devastating defeat. He was drowning in an ocean of Turmoil. Yet the flotation device, that kept him afloat, was his tight grasp on the ***Word of God***, the ***Promises of God***, ***the Love of God*** and the ***Favor of God***!

He desires that everyone could experience this peace - this place of rest in their ***turbulent times.***

ARK Angel Manifesto is a reality check, a challenge, an encouragement and an invitation to be part of the glorious solution for a world in need!

Bring Rob to your organization or church!

For more information on
REFRESH Your LIFE International,
Contact Robert Klassen at
info.refreshyourlife@gmail.com